THE FREEMAN BIGFOOT FILES

MICHAEL FREEMAN

HANGAR 1 PUBLISHING

Table of Contents

This book is dedicated to my father, Paul Freeman.
May he someday get the recognition he so rightfully deserves.
I hope this would make him proud. This is for you, dad.
To my mother Nancy, whose love and devotion never wavered.
She will always be a beacon of light that will forever be missed.
And to my boys, Grant, Lennox, and Finnian.
Though you never got to meet your Grandpa, I'm sure he sees you every
day. May you have this to hold onto, always.

I would like to give a special thank you to my wife Whitney, the backbone
of our family and a beautiful mother to our children. To her family, and her
mother Judy. To my brother Duane and his family, my sister Linda and my
nephew Cody. And to Karin Perkins and her family. This is my family.

I would also like to thank the following people for their contributions to, and
help on this work: Cliff Barackman, Dr. Jeff Meldrum, Thom Powell,
Johnathan C Sumerlin, Dar Glasgow Addington, Jeff Menz, Todd Prescott, Dr.
Russ Jones, Gene Robinson, Larry Lund, Alex Hajicek, Blane Hajicek, and to Doug
Hajicek, thank you for your dedication sir, you certainly made this possible.

AUTHOR'S NOTE

There are a few subjects I would like to address before you fully open this book. I will do so in hope of eliminating any questions that may arise during your experience.

I know there will be some who wonder "why me and why now?" Why has it taken so long to do something that by all rights deserved to be done years ago? And why is Michael Freeman the one doing it? The answer to both of those questions is simple yet complex. This book is being done now because I wasn't ready to do it before. There wasn't enough information that had been put together to form an accurate picture, and I didn't have the right people around me to help with and support this project. I have one shot at doing this for my father, and it took me time to be ready. Now for the simple part, maybe. Why me? Honestly, I'm doing this because I'm the only one who wanted to, and in a way, maybe the only one who could.

There is no doubt whatsoever in my mind that the biggest question that will come out of this book will be, "Where is Duane?" By my own admission, I will admit that maybe he should have been the person to have written this book. He was older and more involved in the research for a number of years. He was also more exposed to the ridicule. We all have our own feelings toward the media as well as the Bigfoot community as a whole, or even individuals within that. My brother is a private person, and Duane Freeman declined to be a part of this project. Therefore, I have done my best to include him and represent how important he was in the early years of my father's research.

The Database as you will see referred to many times is the evidence that has been collected and catalogued. Not just of Paul Freeman, but all known evidence. If something is said to be in the database that means that we know of the evidence, and it has been recorded and documented with the best information we currently have so it may be further analyzed.

A point was made from the beginning of this project to not speak ill of anyone, though there were opportunities to do such. I believe that this is all too common within the Bigfoot community and the research field as well, and I will have no part in it. This should, after all, be a concentrated effort working toward a common goal, and not a jealousy contest.

Lastly, I would like to say that the views and opinions expressed within may not coincide with yours, and that is alright. We all have the right to our own beliefs, and it should be such. Take the information provided to you and do with it as you will. I only hope that I have been able to give you something to think about and enjoy and that I have successfully been able to provide you with not only scientific evidence and research but also the story of a man.

A unique feature we have added is the use of QR Codes. Readers will find these located throughout the book. Each QR Code will allow you, the reader, the ability to scan each one using the camera feature on your mobile device. From there, your mobile device will immediately link to other fascinating videos, audio, images, or more information on the given section of the book.

My Name is Paul Freeman

INTRODUCTION

My name is Michael Freeman. I am the son of Paul Freeman, and I would like to tell you about how special this book is. Not only is it about my father, but it is also very special and unique in its' own way. This project was a labor of love, and also of some frustration. My father's evidence was well documented for the time, and in great part due to my mother and her dedication to doing such. But nonetheless, there were still some mysteries to be solved, and gaps that needed to be filled. I would not have been able to do either without the help of the individuals who contributed to this work. I have brought together for you some of the most respected minds in the field of Bigfoot research. They will provide you with their thoughts and experiences. Some will give you scientific facts.

Also contained in these pages are over one hundred documented photographs from evidence logs, and my father's own personal photo albums. I have written highly detailed captions so these photographs will be as educational as they are interesting. But what makes this book even more unique is that I have also provided you with video and audio clips from my father's own personal recordings. Most of what's contained within this book has never been seen or heard before, until now. So whenever you see one of the QR codes like the one at the bottom of this page, just take out your smartphone, open the camera, and use it to scan that code. Then watch and listen as something magical begins to happen. The audio tapes contained in this book were made by my father in private between 1988 and 1995. They were done so with the intention of writing his own book about his life, and his search for bigfoot. Unfortunately, that's not a dream he was able to realize before his life came to an end. But in the words of Jim Croce, and one of my father's favorite songs, "I've got a name. And I carry it with me like my daddy did, but I'm living the dream that he can't live". So although this is light years from what he most likely imagined, this is, after all, Paul Freeman's book. Now go ahead, give it a try, and I will let my father get us started in his own words.

My Name is Paul Freeman

"Likely the best Sasquatch tracker of all time"
-Thom Powell

Photo courtesy of Thom Powell.

*June 26th, 1982. Paul poses with the Hyampom cast from Bob Titmus.
Photo courtesy of the estate of Bob Titmus.*

I.

BIGFOOT OF THE BLUES

Jeff Meldrum

My first specific introduction to Paul Freeman came when Richard Greenwell, Secretary of the International Society of Cryptozoology, asked me to review a booklet penned by an outdoor reporter and columnist Vance Orchard, of Walla Walla, Washington, entitled *Bigfoot of the Blues* (1993), referring to the Blue Mountains extending north from Oregon to the east of Walla Walla, and on towards the Snake River. Vance's columns often featured developments relating to Bigfoot, a keen interest of his. Paul's exploits were frequently featured, along with other personalities, such as Wes Sumerlin and Bill Laughery. As I reviewed the book, I compiled a list of highlighted characters that I hoped to get more familiar with. Vance was very helpful, providing contact information for all. Through conversations and correspondence, I began to gain an appreciation of the context and backdrop for Paul's claims of discovering evidence of and even having encounters with Bigfoot. There remained red flags and some incredulity. After all, if sasquatch exist, they must be extremely rare and reclusive to have remained unacknowledged by science for all this time. Most reported encounters or discoveries of footprints are rather singular and almost entirely chance circumstances. Any claim to not only multiple footprint finds, but also repeat encounters with the trackmakers seemed contrary to this "norm."

With this preparation, a serendipitous and fortuitous opportunity was realized. With my curiosity in sasquatch rekindled by recent experiences, my brother, Michael, and I had made a little road trip from Boise to Pullman to visit Dr. Grover Krantz in his lab to examine his footprint cast collection, in February of 1996. This proved especially enlightening since a significant portion of the collection consisted of replicas of footprint casts originally collected by Paul Freeman, as well as other examples from the Blues documented by Sumerlin, Laughery, and others. On our return to Boise, we decided to take an alternate route diverting through Walla Walla and paid a surprise visit to Paul Freeman. We arrived at his house as he was just pulling into the driveway. He cordially invited us in and generously made his casts available for examination. Pressing him with questions about the details of the casts, he finally said, "Well you obviously know a lot about footprints, would you like to see some fresh tracks?" It turned out he had found some that very morning prior to our arrival. He made a practice of running the dirt roads in the Blues for a sign, beginning as soon as the snows had receded from the foothills. These were the first tracks of the season. I thought to myself, *"What do we have to lose?"* and agreed to take a look. What we observed and the implications are spelled out more fully in my book, *Sasquatch: Legend Meets Science*. In short, this experience altered the course of my career, resonating over much of the next three decades.

This region presents an interesting setting. This part of the Blue Mountains forms a dog-leg projecting from the main body of the range in eastern Oregon. In contrast to the surrounding sagebrush steppe, the elevations form a rain trap catching the westerlies laden with moisture from the Pacific Ocean. This precipitation supports a montane forest habitat with a productive understory and charges a system of springs, even where the lesser elevations lack persistent winter snowpack. On its western slopes, the Mill Creek watershed serves as the municipal water supply for Walla Walla and is therefore fenced off with restricted access maintained by the USFS. This area of isolation has taken on a certain air of mystery and is perceived by some as a sasquatch refuge and haven of sorts. This may be true in part, but the real "haven" includes the extensive Wenaha-Tucannon wilderness encompassing nearly 180,000 acres. It is a roadless area abutting the watershed and extending towards Idaho's Hell Canyon. The Blues support a variety of wildlife, including one of the largest elk herds in the lower forty-eight.

Another feature of this region that contributes to the inordinate number of footprints reportedly discovered, is the high loess content of the soil. Loess is Pleistocene sediment with the consistency of flour. it is sometimes called glacial flour. Whether dry or wet, the fine particle size of this sediment means that it picks up remarkable detail in footprints, including skin ridge detail, or dermatoglyphics. Add to this the fact that many of the roads in the region are little more than graded tracks, with no roadbed improvements. In the absence of gravel roadbeds, these tertiary roads, exposing the Palouse loess deposits, make excellent track beds for recording spoor of wildlife crossing or walking along them. It seems the rare sasquatch are no exception if Freeman's 10 years of casting and mapping tracks are to be taken seriously.

There is a remarkable polarity in opinion surrounding Paul's evidence. On the one hand, there are the skeptics/critics, such as Joel Hardin, US Border Patrol agent, and Peter Byrne, adventurer and Bigfoot/yeti investigator. Hardin was the US border patrol tracker called in by the USFS to investigate the initial encounter reported by Freeman. From the outset, Hardin betrayed a skepticism about sasquatch and participated in conversations to that effect even before his examination of the trackway, as reported by Rene Dahinden. Hardin's report clearly reinforced his training and bias as a man-tracker, with a narrow frame of reference for interpreting signs of human gait patterns and footprints. His criticisms of the trackway highlighted the very contrasts one might expect for a large heavy bipedal non-human hominoid -- e.g., a flat arch-less foot, lacking differential plantar pressure points beneath heel and ball, the more consistent step length accompanying a compliant gait. His observations were spot on, but his interpretations were not. He devoted an entire chapter to his misapprehension of the foot[print evidence (Hardin, 2004). Peter Byrne, a long-time investigator of Bigfoot and former director of the *Bigfoot Research Center*, dismissed the tracks I documented in 1996, which were shown to me by Freeman, suggesting they might be bear tracks. He went on to opine in print that the Blue Mountains seemed to be a likely habitat for sasquatch, but then made the inexplicable assertion that no credible evidence had ever been discovered there (Byrne, 2013).

On the other hand, it is noteworthy that the collected materials from the Blues have been examined by more doctorates than any other body of Bigfoot data. The footprint evidence collected by Freeman and other investigators was at the core of Dr. Grover Krantz's analysis and figured prominently in his book, *Big Footprints* (1992). Krantz was the first to publish on the observation of dermatoglyphics present on some casts of footprints from this collection. Dr. Henner Fahrenbach studied the hair evidence from the Blues and established what has been referred to as the "gold standard" for sasquatch hair attribution based on distinctive criteria repeated throughout North America. I first documented examples of the midtarsal break from examples present among the footprints examined at Five-points, outside Walla Walla. This feature figures prominently in the description and diagnosis of the ichnotaxon for sasquatch footprints, *Anthropoidipes ameriborealis* (Meldrum, 2007). Others, such as Dr. Ron Brown, Dr. John Bindernagel, and Dr. George Schaller have favorably examined footprint evidence from the region.

Freeman managed to capture a video clip of an encounter, which in some respects rivals the Patterson-Gimlin film. Investigating footprints found at Deduct Spring, Freeman first videoed a set of footprints approximately 13 inches in length, which bear a remarkable resemblance to the footprints I examined in 1996, not far removed at Five-points. Then sounds of brush popping alerted him to the approach of a sasquatch. A figure very reminiscent of "Patty", the subject of the P-G film, makes its way across the frame, then vanishes into the underbrush. Relative to features in the background (a standing snag and a fir tree) later measured by investigators, the height is estimated at approximately 7 feet. Its reaction is startled, but quite natural as it pauses under partial cover to glare back at Freeman before hastily exiting the scene. A parting shot reveals what appears to be an infant scooped up from the ground and clutched to the creature's side, before disappearing from sight into the forest.

The possible existence of relict hominoids has gained some recognition as a legitimate question of human evolution. The paradigm in anthropology that has for decades conceived of the emergence of the hominin lineage as a rather singular event, an "exclusive club" accommodating only one species occupying a specialized niche, has been ousted by the ever-growing assemblage of fossil hominin species. Not only has the hominin family tree taken on a very bushy appearance, but many parallel branches to our own have persisted until far more recently —mere tens of thousands of years ago — than would have been recognized even a few decades ago. The proposition that a few of these species may have survived into the present is a very real possibility, worthy of serious consideration and active investigation. However, the accumulating evidence of survival – footprints, hair, photos, eyewitness encounters, indigenous folklore – some of the most compelling originating from Paul Freeman's investigations in the Blue Mountains, remains inconclusive short of a physical body. It is largely dismissed out of hand by the mainstream, without receiving objective consideration. The affirmative opinions of a growing list of experts are generally discounted, even if they manage to obtain an academic platform to present their analyses of the data.

This photo of Paul, taken in Camas, Washington, in 1984, shows him holding a cast from 1982 and a painting he did of Bigfoot.

2.
MY VERY OWN SUPERMAN

Michael Freeman

I don't need someone to kill one and show me a body, and I don't need to see one for myself. I have all the proof I will ever need for the existence of Bigfoot, and I found it thirty years ago. I was fifteen years old on August 20th, 1992 when my dad came home from Deduct Spring Oregon, in the Blue Mountains. You could hear him come through the door. Hell, you could feel him come through the door. I was downstairs in our basement with a few of my friends when we heard him yelling for my mother, and I very much doubt that anyone there will ever forget that afternoon. My father was agitated. He was shaking, dirty, and sweaty, and he was scared. Paul Freeman was superman. At least that's what he was to me when I was a child. He was big and tough. He was strong, and he was brave. I never knew my father to be afraid of any man or beast on this planet. I was with my dad the morning he died, and even then, the only time in my life that I ever saw him scared of anything was that day. And that right there is the only proof that I will ever need for the existence of Bigfoot. I know they are real, I saw it in his eyes.

"You could drop me off in Mexico in my underwear, and I would show up in Canada wearing a Polar Bear coat" - Paul Freeman

There are a thousand stories about my dad. I can remember listening to tales of superhuman exploits that you wouldn't even believe could take place in a movie. I would hear them from my uncle Larry Cochran, my father's best friend for many years. Sometimes they were from one of his hunting or work buddies, or even from my dad himself. Often my mother would interject and say something funny the boys had forgotten about, as she knew the stories as good or better than they did, having heard them at least a hundred times. Even my brother Duane still spins a tale or two when we get together, and I now find myself starting to share these stories with my own boys.

I can remember my excitement as a child listening to the story of the five-hundred-pound bear that fell at their feet when my brother was twelve and his gun jammed. My dad patiently waiting for him to get it worked out until he could wait no more. Finally, he put one center shot in the heart of the beast, now only a mere ten yards from them, and rising to its hind legs, roaring. The bear took enough steps before its body finally gave out to nearly land on them as my dad stood like a statue, the beast falling stone dead. That is a true story. There is the tale of the trophy Elk in the Cascade Mountains that he could not get a clear shot on, so he took off following its tracks through the snow, up over the mountain, and pursued it until it ran itself into the ground. Exhausted and no longer able to run, he was able to walk right up to it, steam blowing from its nostrils, and put it down. That might be a true story, At least halfway.

According to my brother Duane, it is very likely to be rooted in a solid truth. Apparently, my dad ripped the door off of a car one time when a man insulted my mother. Yes, I actually believe that one. He was a renowned tough guy, a former boxer and bouncer, and he worked as a bodyguard for both Ricky Nelson and Chuck Berry when they would come to Washington and Oregon to do concerts. Anyone who would have insulted my mother in front of my father would have had a death wish. Let us not forget about the time in 1990, when he sent his thirteen-year-old son down the bottom of a small canyon and into a thicket of trees. He wanted me to flush out a black bear that had gone in there so he could get a clean shot as it came out the other side.

I clearly remember his instructions to me as they were as follows: walk heavy to make as much noise as you can and he will come out the other side. If it does turn on you, shoot once so I know, and then turn around and run back the way you came as fast as you can. I'll drop the son of a bitch as soon as his head comes out. We ate bear for a month. I never even made it to the bottom of that canyon or even close to that thicket of trees. I heard the shot when I was halfway down. But there was never a question of whether or not I would have entered that thicket had it not come out simply due to my approach. Of course, I would have. His word was law in that environment. There has never been anyone you would trust more.

I don't think there is a person out there who ever met my dad that doesn't have some kind of story to tell. The man was larger than life, in both stature, and personality. He was a generous man and would give you the shirt off of his back if you needed it. My dad was open to talking to anyone about his experiences or giving them advice, and despite his intimidating stature, he was friendly and easily approachable. He set up displays on Bigfoot at the local malls and became known for giving away copies of casts, photos and sometimes even a hair sample. On more than one occasion he went to talk with kids at one of the local elementary schools, even helping a couple with projects on the subject. Once he even took a few kids on a mini Bigfoot expedition in the Blues for fun.

My parents' home was a friendly and open sanctuary. Both my dad and my mother were well liked by all my friends growing up, and even after I had graduated high school and left for college there were a few friends of mine that would still stop by to say hi to my mom and dad, and of course, stay for dinner. At least one of my good friends also spent a night or two there, sleeping one off after drinking a bit too much, and not being able to make it safely back to their own home. Or maybe they simply did not want their mother to see them in such a state. They knew that if you got a hold of the Freemans, Paul would make sure you were alright. My dad was generous, and he was kind. But make no mistake about it, he would also bury you in a cave in those mountains if you harmed his family.

The Mall

Paul Freeman was a meat cutter by trade, but he was born an outdoorsman. And he wasn't always a Bigfoot tracker, although that is what he is best known for. Believe it or not, he wasn't one to believe in Bigfoot or such things like that. Having spent a good majority of his life in the mountains, he had never come across anything that he couldn't explain. He was a man that knew every animal in the forest, he knew their tracks and their sounds. He knew every berry and mushroom that you could eat, and he knew the ones that would make you sick, or even kill you. Stories of monsters in those woods were just that, stories passed around by drunk cowboys and loggers who had taken too many blows to the head. My dad never set out to find Bigfoot, nor did he set out to dedicate his life to trying to prove their existence. But nonetheless, Bigfoot ended up changing his life whether he wanted it to or not.

I was five years old when my dad had that first encounter that would change him forever. We had just moved from Camas, Washington to Milton-Freewater Oregon, a small town just across the state line from Walla Walla, Washington where my dad had taken a new job. On June 10th, 1982 my father was on patrol, working for the Forest Service in the Blue Mountains of the Umatilla National Forest.

Job Description

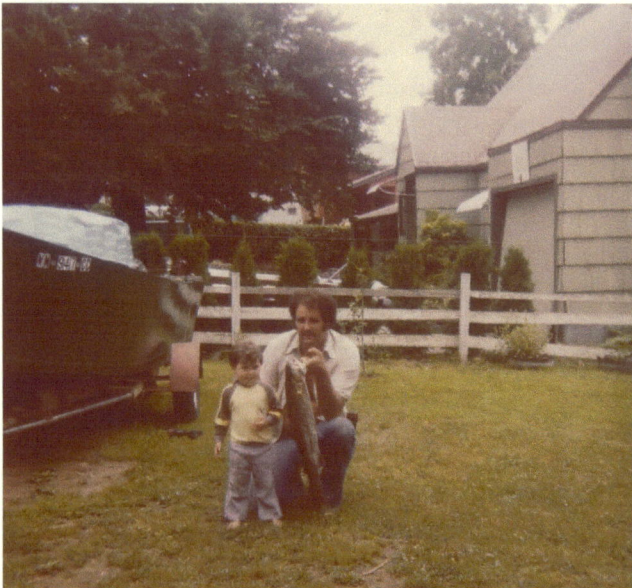

Paul and youngest son Michael. Camas, Washington, 1980.

Paul Freeman at the John Day Rodeo in John Day, Oregon 1963.

The inspection of a track. I believe this to be Bill Laughery. Date and location are unknown at this time.

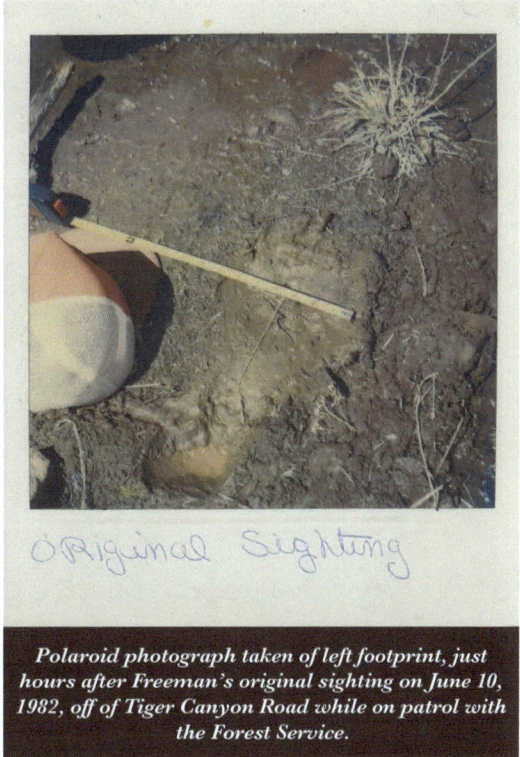

ORiginal Sighting

Polaroid photograph taken of left footprint, just hours after Freeman's original sighting on June 10, 1982, off of Tiger Canyon Road while on patrol with the Forest Service.

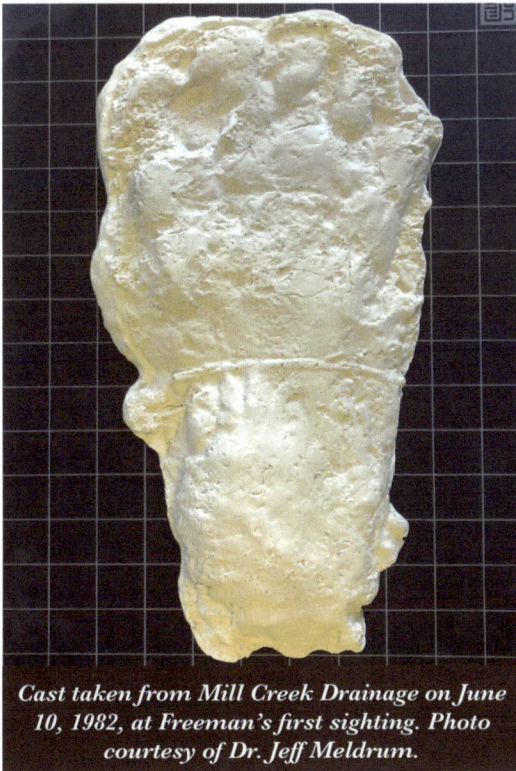

Cast taken from Mill Creek Drainage on June 10, 1982, at Freeman's first sighting. Photo courtesy of Dr. Jeff Meldrum.

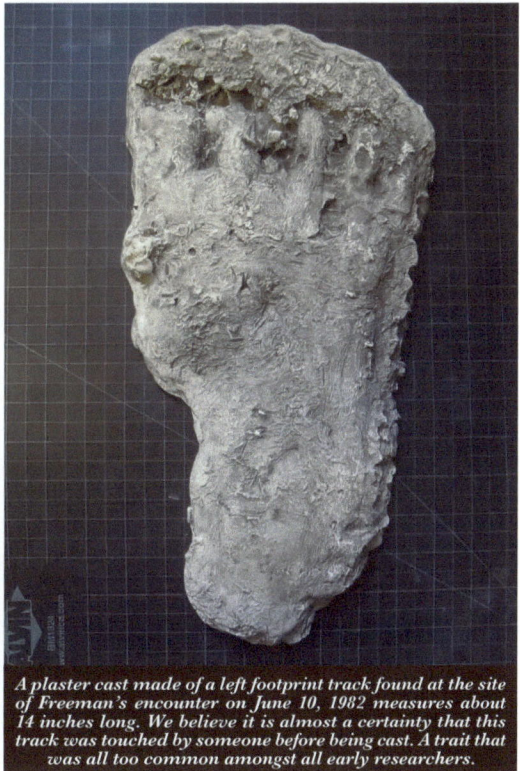

A plaster cast made of a left footprint track found at the site of Freeman's encounter on June 10, 1982 measures about 14 inches long. We believe it is almost a certainty that this track was touched by someone before being cast. A trait that was all too common amongst all early researchers.

Watershed patrolman:

I saw bigfoot

By VANCE ORCHARD
Of the Union-Bulletin

Bigfoot lives!

At least Paul Freeman says it does. Freeman, a Mill Creek Watershed patrolman, claims he saw what looked like a bigfoot, acted like a bigfoot and even smelled like a bigfoot Thursday noon.

Freeman says he sighted one of the legendary hairy beasts near the top of Tiger Canyon Road, about three-fourths of a mile above the road to the North Fork Walla Walla River.

And, before anyone dismisses Freeman's claims, one might want to take a look at the plaster casts of footprints

It was probably about nine feet tall, with dark, reddish-black hair all over its body, Freeman said. Long arms hung to its knees as the creature walked away in a slouching manner.

taken shortly after Freeman reported the sighting.

The cast measures 14 inches long and 7½ inches at the widest part. Wayne Long of the U.S. Forest Service notes that Freeman's weight — 265 pounds — did not depress the soil of the road as did that of the maker of the prints.

"Freeman didn't sink into the dirt at all," said Long.

Freeman was walking a portion of the watershed boundary on the old logging spur roadway when he smelled something amiss.

"A very bad odor hung in the air, but I thought nothing of it at the time."

Then, about 50 yards down the road, he said the creature came down a steep bank toward him.

Freeman thought the creature was coming for him, so he turned and ran up the road. But, turning to look back, he found the creature going the other way — apparently startled at seeing Freeman.

The last thing Freeman, a veteran hunter and trapper in the Blue Mountains, saw of the bigfoot it was walking around a bend of the road toward the confines of the watershed.

Freeman, a 39-year-old Milton-Freewater resident who started his watershed patrol duty May 1, stands 6-5. The creature, he said, towered over him. It was probably about nine feet tall, with dark, reddish-black hair all over its body. Long arms hung to its knees as the creature walked away in a slouching manner, he said.

His reported sighting isn't the first recorded in recent years in the Blue Mountains, but it is the first in daylight and with such clarity.

Pete Luther saw footprints that measured 19 inches long and eight inches wide, spaced five feet apart while he and another cyclist were riding a trail bike on the Tiger Canyon Road in 1966. Roger Patterson, the man who later claimed he captured a bigfoot on film, came here to investigate, but an overnight rain wiped out the evidence. Patterson, then the leading "tracker" of the bigfoot, was convinced the creature had been here.

ORiginal Sighting

In 1970, near Camp Kiwanis on the Mill Creek Road, Rich Myers of Walla Walla reported seeing "something" loom up in the dusk in the brush at the side of the road. As it screamed a high-pitched sound, Myers took off on his motorcycle.

Henry Avery, Route 1, saw "something large and hairy" at his house in 1974. The creature struck his house and strode over the fence as Avery fired four shots at it.

In 1970, Fred McPherson, a farm mechanic, heard sounds unlike any animal he had ever heard in the upper Coppei Creek drainage.

But before curiosity-seekers begin making plans to head up to the watershed to try and spot a bigfoot, Long warns that the area is restricted and access forbidden except for limited hunting by special permits in the fall.

An article by Vance Orchard on Paul's original encounter in 1982.

Photo taken June 10, 1982, at the site of encounter.

Left foot from wet trackway found after Freeman's sighting.

Trackway running across the logging road Freeman was using at the time of his encounter on June 10, 1982.

This shoe was placed next to a track for size comparison, notice the vast difference in the width of the foot compared to that of the shoe.

Another angle from Tiger Canyon showing multiple steps in the trackway found at Paul Freeman's original sighting.

This photo taken in 1987 shows Paul at the location the animal stepped off the hill and into the road during his initial encounter on June 10, 1982.

June 10th, 1982 excellent close view of the left and right tracks taken at original sighting.

My dad was on foot, as he had gotten out of his service vehicle to track a herd of elk, and was hoping to get a head count on calves that day. The first thing he noticed as he started around a bend, cresting a small hill in an old logging road was the smell, and then he came face to face with something he couldn't explain.

The Smell

He would tell you he knew instantly that it wasn't a bear. As the hair on the nape of my father's neck and arms stood on end, he watched it cross the road and turn to look at him. He was close enough to see the muscles in its chest and stomach moving as it took in breaths. He could hear it making a low, guttural growl. He watched it walk the length of at least two football fields, pausing more than once to look back at him before it disappeared over a hill. It walked leaning slightly forward, and not once as my father watched it did it ever straighten out its knees. No, this was not a bear, this was nothing he had ever seen. The first thought that crossed his mind was that of a prehistoric man, but even at fifty to sixty yards away it seemed to tower over him.

Sighting 82

My dad made it to a ranger station and called in what he had just seen. As he waited for his superiors to arrive, he and another employee named Dave headed back to the site. It is worth noting here that in Freeman's interviews he comments that he wasn't particularly surprised by the smell, though it did make him want to turn his head away. He describes it as having the odor of something dead, but musky like urine. His lack of surprise could be attributed to his initial thinking that he may have come across the decaying body of a mentally disabled boy that had gone missing during a family picnic in the area some months prior. Or that possibly he was nearing a dead carcass of some other wildlife not yet taken back by the forest.

Helicopter

An investigation was done, casts of footprints were made, and photos of tracks were taken. A Search and Rescue team was called in to assist as well. Wayne Long, a superior of Paul's at the Forest Service, and one of the individuals who went back to

Dropped keys

Crazy

investigate the area noted that Paul, even at six foot five inches and nearly two hundred sixty pounds, barely made an indentation in the soil around where the creature had walked and left tracks.

It was only six days later that he and a fellow employee, Bill Epoch, would find and cast the dermal prints a few miles away at a place called Elk Wallow, at the bottom of Low Canyon. Two separate sets of tracks were found there. The first are thought to belong to the same animal my dad encountered less than a week earlier. The second set, belonging to a new and unseen creature, left tracks that would produce what we now call the Paul Freeman Dermals.

June 16

The Rock Print found at Elk Wallow on June 16th, 1982.

Close-up of Rock print.

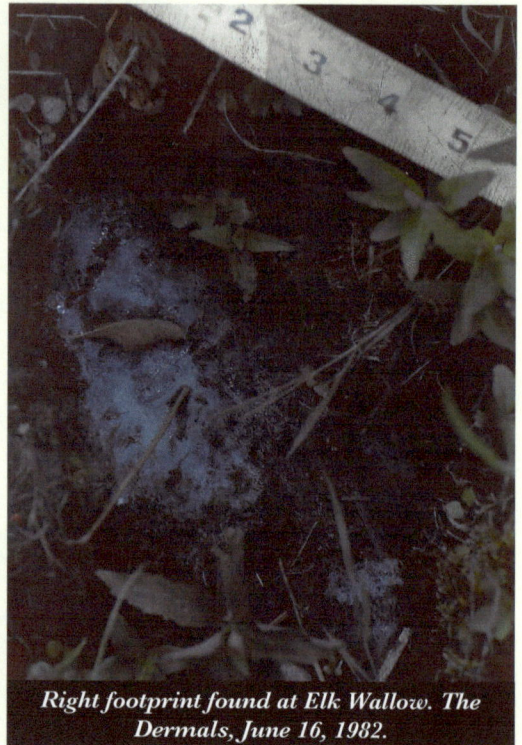

Right footprint found at Elk Wallow. The Dermals, June 16, 1982.

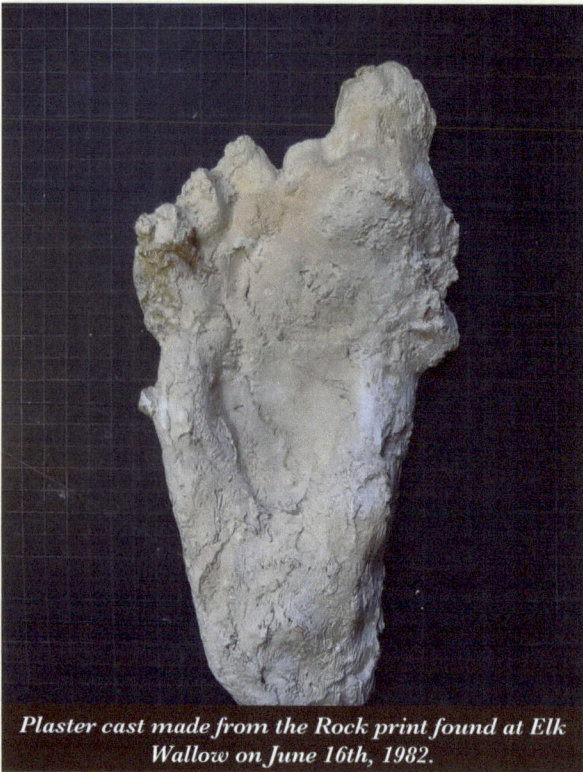

One of the tracks from the Elk Wallow trackway.

Plaster cast made from the Rock print found at Elk Wallow on June 16th, 1982.

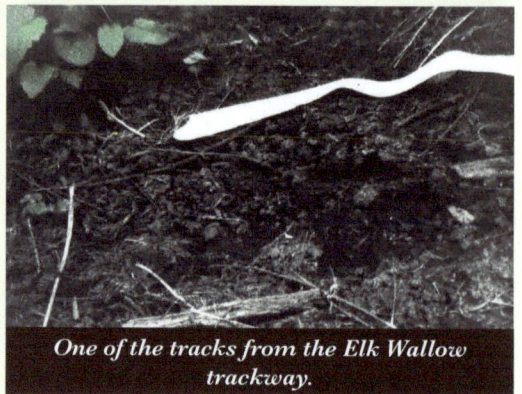

Another view of the Rock print found at Elk Wallow on June16th, 1982.

June 16, 1982, at Elk Wallow.

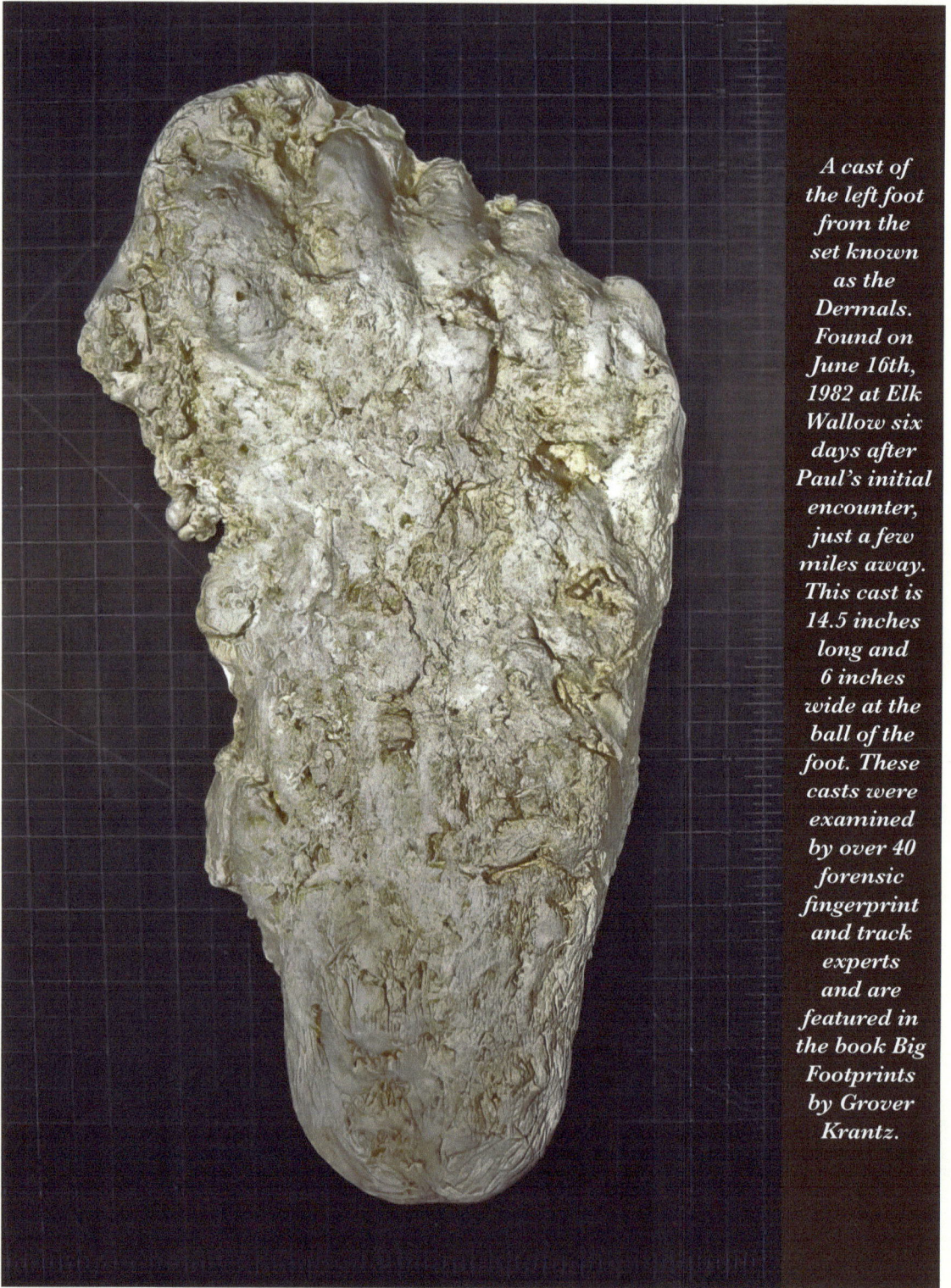

A cast of the left foot from the set known as the Dermals. Found on June 16th, 1982 at Elk Wallow six days after Paul's initial encounter, just a few miles away. This cast is 14.5 inches long and 6 inches wide at the ball of the foot. These casts were examined by over 40 forensic fingerprint and track experts and are featured in the book Big Footprints by Grover Krantz.

This footprint found at Elk Wallow, known as the left Dermal, would become one of the most important Bigfoot tracks ever found.

A close-up of dermatoglyphics on the left foot.

Elk Wallow June 16, 1982. The Dermals.

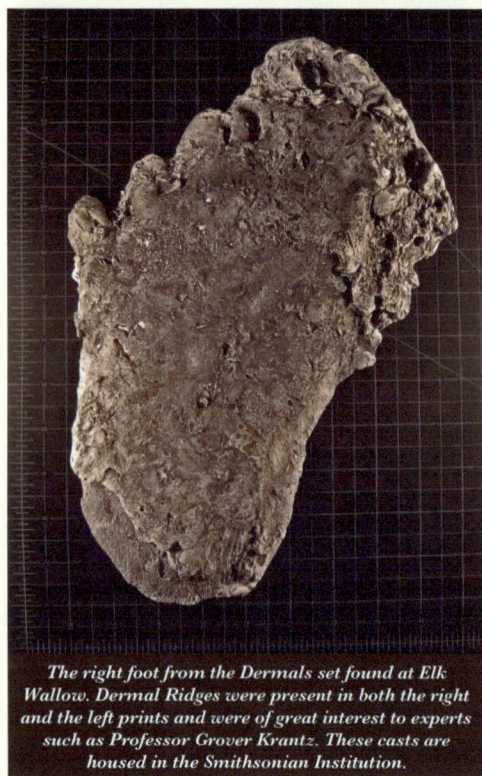

The right foot from the Dermals set found at Elk Wallow. Dermal Ridges were present in both the right and the left prints and were of great interest to experts such as Professor Grover Krantz. These casts are housed in the Smithsonian Institution.

The Dermals.

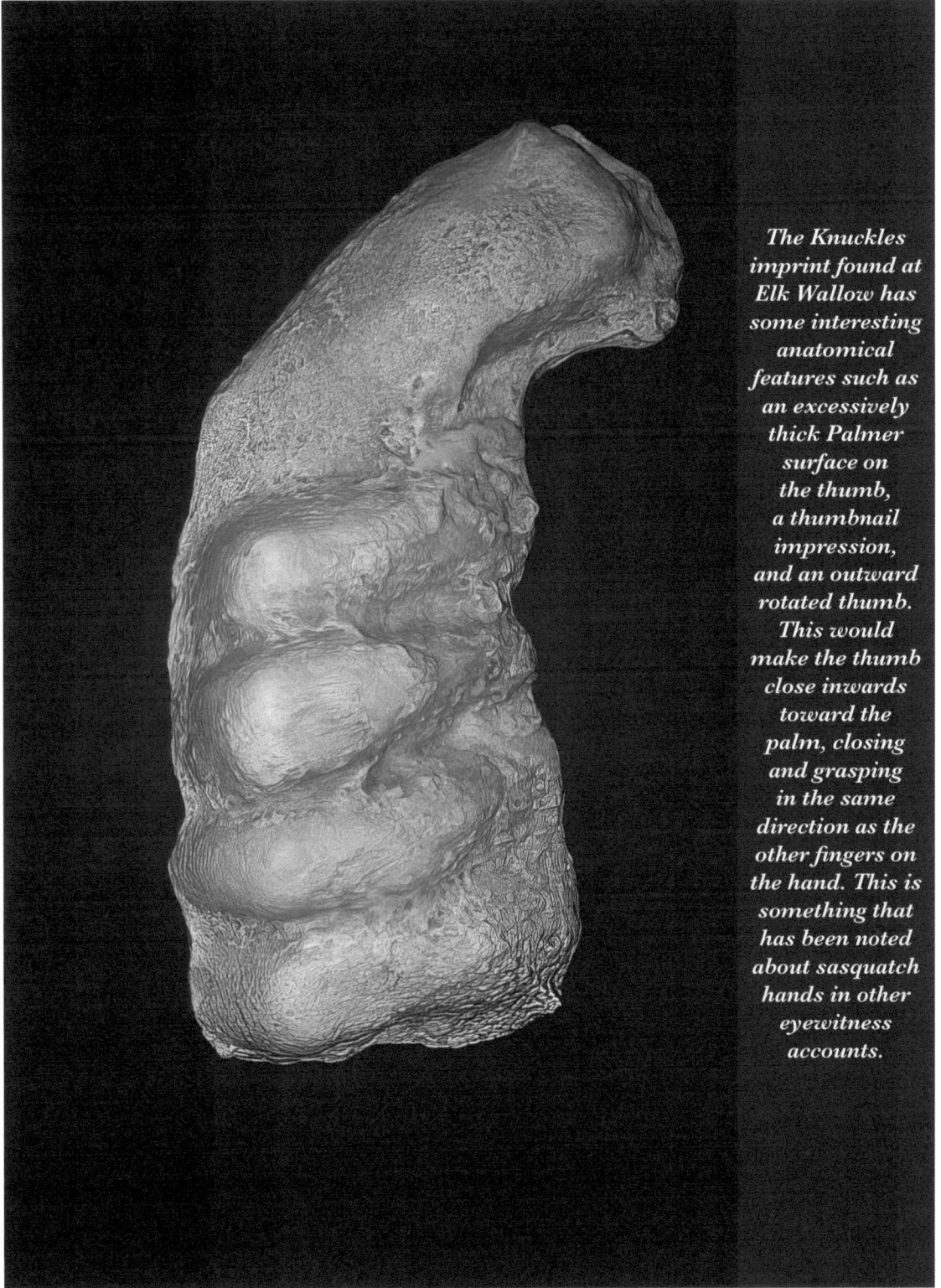

The Knuckles imprint found at Elk Wallow has some interesting anatomical features such as an excessively thick Palmer surface on the thumb, a thumbnail impression, and an outward rotated thumb. This would make the thumb close inwards toward the palm, closing and grasping in the same direction as the other fingers on the hand. This is something that has been noted about sasquatch hands in other eyewitness accounts.

Another track from the Dermals found by Paul Freeman at Elk Wallow.

Paul Freeman with Ted Butters and Bob Titmus. June 26th, 1982. Photo courtesy of the estate of Bob Titmus.

Those were a big deal, hell they still are a big deal. Professor Grover Krantz would rave about them, and as a matter of fact, the casts of those tracks have been kept in the Smithsonian Institution for many years now.

We ended up moving again shortly after the Dermals were found. I won't get into the specifics of what happened between my dad and the Forest Service, it's a bit of he said she said to be honest, but he always claimed the pressure and the ridicule forced him away. There were crank calls, and accusations ranging from being drunk to just plain crazy. There was also a bit of vandalism to our home. Those days were just different in a small town. I think that the pressure and the ridicule forced my mom away, and he went with her. Maybe we will never fully know, and honestly, that's just fine with me. My Grandmother Margaret Cochran (my mother's mother) had also died during this time period and left her home in Camas to my mother. This provided another reason to leave, and a new home to live in.

Krantz1

Broken Foot

I can faintly remember packing our bags in 1982 and going back to what I knew as home. Living in my Grandmother's house was strange. I was always scared of the basement, even when she was alive, and I swear to this day that house on Benton Street was haunted. My brother has even told me that he thought he saw our Grandma once, in the hallway between what used to be her bedroom and the hall bathroom. I had started kindergarten during this time, in 1983 at Dorothy Fox Elementary. My parents had opened a successful business, a deli and smoked meats shop aptly named FREEMANS. I often think of what it would have been like if that would have been the end of all this Bigfoot business.

Of course, that wasn't the end, the Blue Mountains kept pulling my father back without me even realizing it. I guess I was too young to really understand my dad's weekend trips, and why he was gone so much during those four years we spent back in Camas, Washington. It wasn't until later that I realized what he was doing. He was going back. The man saw something that changed him, and he couldn't stay away.

There were some pieces of important evidence discovered in those missing years. Most notably Wrinkle Foot was found and cast in the Blue Mountains in 1984. Another extraordinary casting in my dad's collection, Wrinkle Foot was named by Professor Krantz, and Its casts are prominently featured in his writings. You will find it in Dr. Meldrum's work as well, and it is one of the most documented individuals in the known database. This is also the time period that my father decided that he was going to kill one. Weekend trips to collect evidence turned into hunting expeditions. Paul Freeman would prove that he was not crazy. He would prove that these creatures do exist and bring a body to the world. Over the next two years that would prove to be exceedingly more difficult than he had ever imagined. A week at a time was spent in the Wenaha Wilderness, away from the prying eyes of the Forest Service, or anyone else for that matter. That is not somewhere you just go. Not down in the Looking Glass area where the ferns are as high as your head, and it is dark at three pm in the canyons. If you don't know what you are doing you won't be coming home.

A Babysitting Situation

Paul showing off the Wrinkle Foot cast set at his home in Camas, Washington, 1984.

Freeman leads an expedition into the Wenaha Wilderness area in 1983.

TERRIFYING

'Bigfoot' altered his life

By MOIRA FARROW

"He looked like prehistoric man walking up that logging spur — all hairy except for his face and chest."

That's how Paul Freeman described his terrifying encounter in a lonely Washington state forest with a creature he believes is the legendary Sasquatch or Bigfoot.

Freeman, a former U.S. Forest Service employee, said in a telephone interview from his Washington home Thursday that the experience has changed his life dramatically.

He claims he quit his job with the forest service when he was harassed by superiors who didn't believe his story. He's now moved to a new job in a different part of the state.

And he's determined to find a Sasquatch next summer to prove its existence to all skeptics.

(U.S. forest service spokesman Dennis Jones said Thursday he "doubted" that Freeman had been harassed and said the forest service believes the incident was a hoax).

Plaster casts of footprints found in the area where Freeman saw the creature were to be presented at a press conference at the University of B.C. today by Dr. Grover Krantz, associate professor of anthropology at Washington State University.

Krantz said earlier this week the footprints are so detailed that he believes they are evidence of the authenticity of the Sasquatch.

"I'm sure proud that Dr. Krantz has backed me up," said Freeman, 39, who now works as a meat cutter in Camas, Wash.

Freeman said he was working for the Walla Walla forest service office last June 10 when he had his controversial encounter.

"It was a beautiful sunny morning and I was about half a mile outside the perimeter of the (Walla Walla) watershed. I got out of my truck because I'd seen some elk on a ridge and I wanted to see if they had any young.

"I walked up an old logging spur which had windfalls over it so I couldn't drive. Suddenly I saw something step off a bank about 10 feet high and down on to the road," he said.

"I saw him about the same time as he saw me. He looked like all the pictures I've seen of prehistoric man. He was real hairy — reddish-brown hair. It was so thick you couldn't see through it on his shoulders, arms and legs. But on his face and chest it was thin enough to see his skin, the color of brown leather."

Feeman said he had never believed in Sasquatch but as he stood staring at the creature —

"I realized it must be a Bigfoot."

"I was about 65 yards away from him and I just stood there looking at him and he looked at me," he said. "I could hear him breathing real heavy as though he'd been running and I could see the muscles in his stomach moving. But that was the only noise he made.

"I was scared and I started backing away a few feet. He made the hair stand up on his neck and shoulders just like a dog does when it tries to frighten someone. . . . When he saw I wasn't coming any further he turned and walked up the road."

Freeman said he phoned for help from a forest service cabin and three colleagues joined him in about 45 minutes. They took photographs and made plaster casts of the creature's footprints.

But Freeman soon ran into problems with supervisors who didn't believe his story.

An article from the Vancouver Sun News 1982.

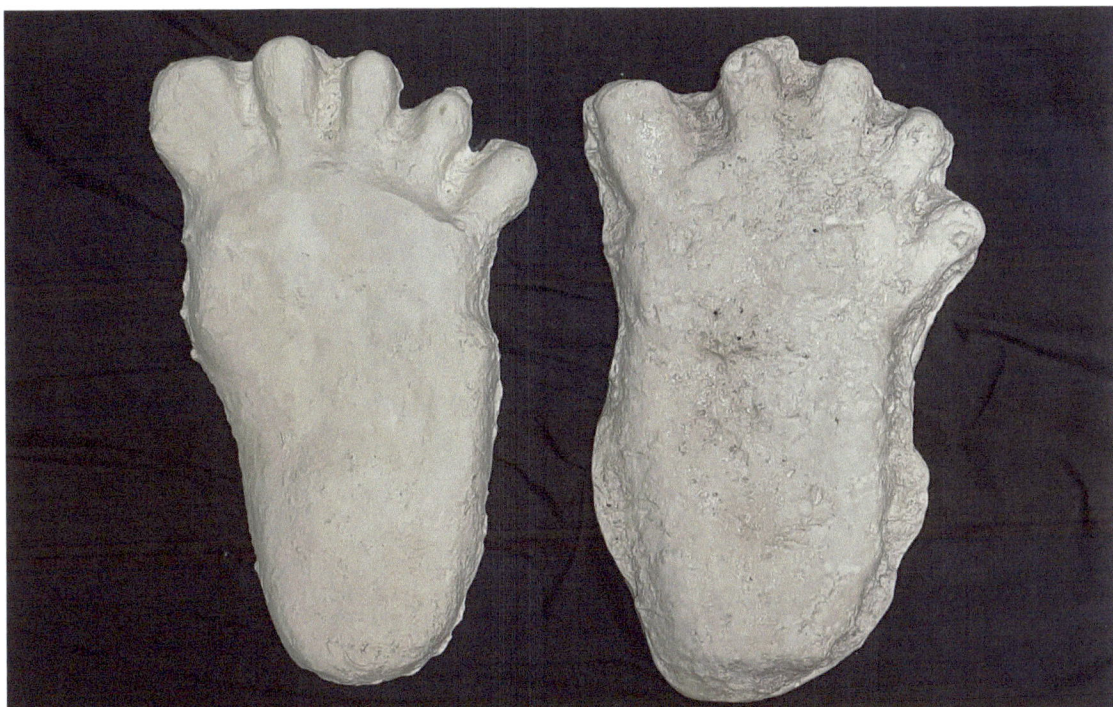

The 1984 left Wrinkle Foot cast with the newly donated 1987 left cast. The toe position is greatly changed on the later cast, but many variables can cause this. Toe shape and length remain greatly similar though and are two of the best indicators in print comparison.

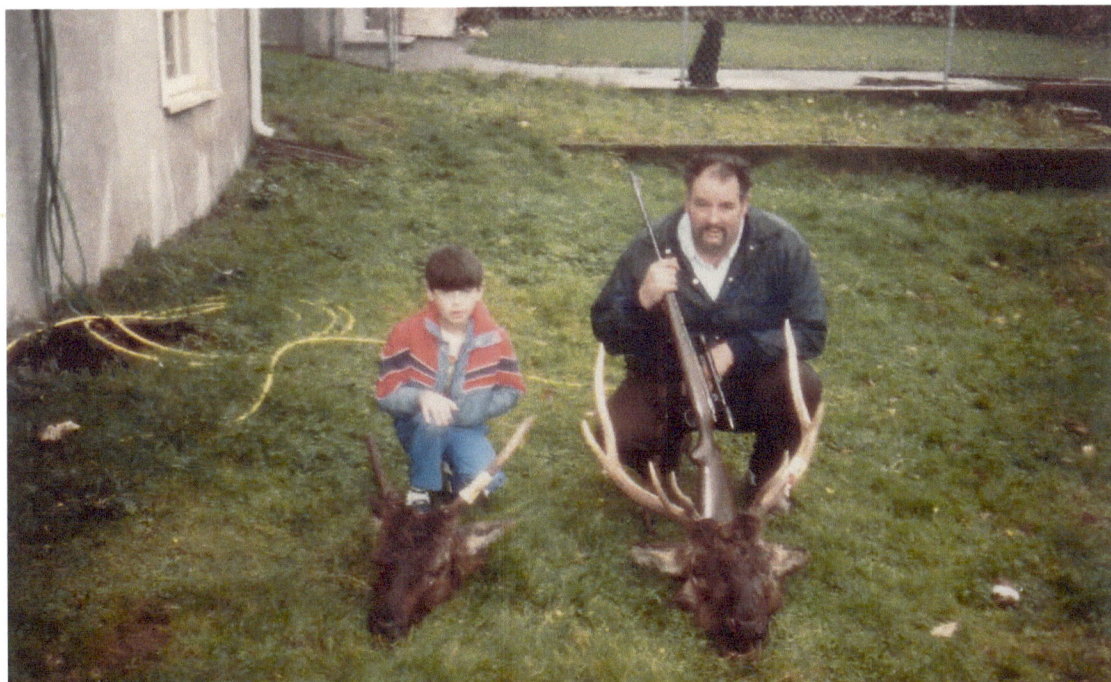

7-year-old Michael and Paul with their recent Elk hunt in Camas, Washington, 1984.

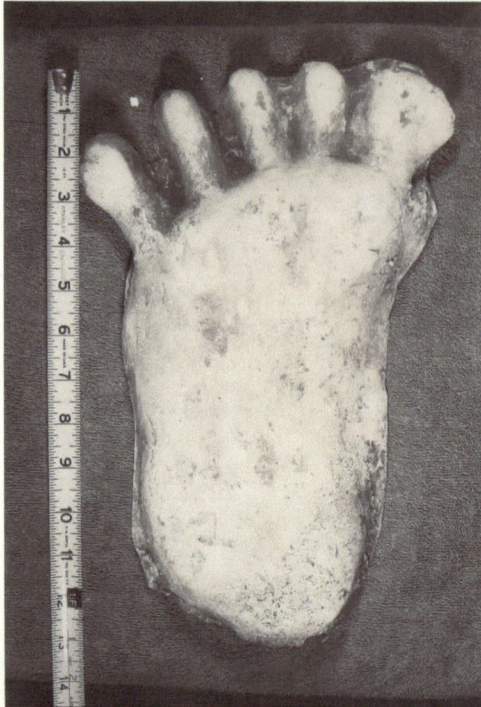

The right Wrinkle Foot cast. These were found and cast in 1984 at a location known as Table Springs. These casts were featured in Grover Krantz's book Big Footprints and were of great interest to the Professor. This animal's casts can also be seen in Dr. Meldrum's book Sasquatch: Legend Meets Science.

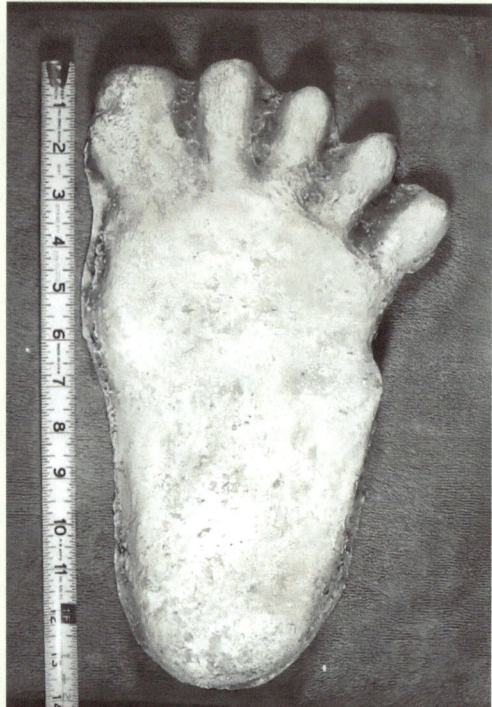

The left foot Wrinkle Foot cast. Notice the wide toe splay on both the left and right prints.

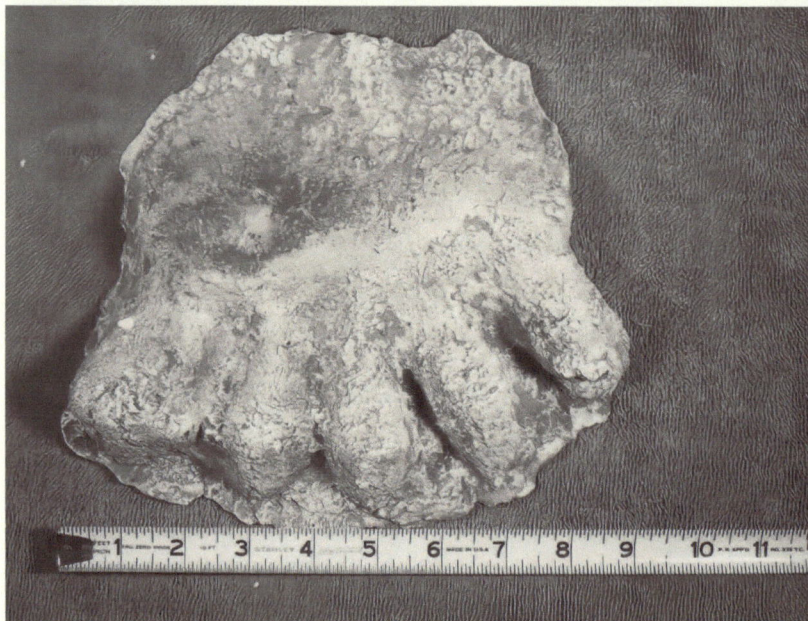

Wrinkle Foot half cast from 1984. Only the front half of the foot, ball and toes, made an impression in the ground as the heel did not come down with weight on this step. The wide toe splay that can be seen on the full left and right casts is also less pronounced on this casting.

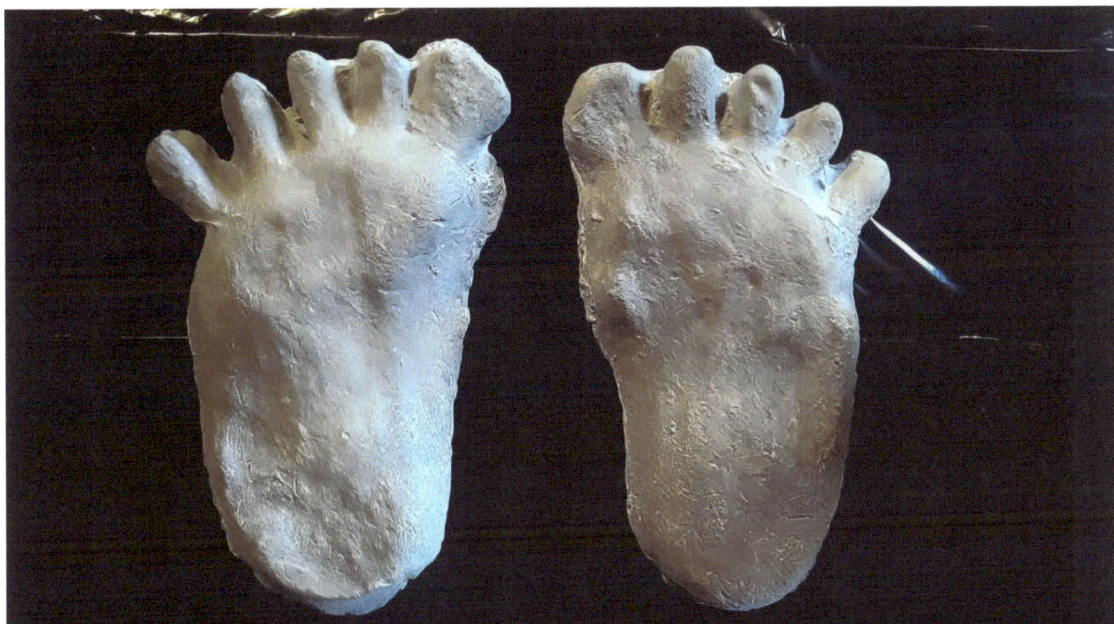

Left and right casts of Wrinkle Foot, side by side. Grover Krantz thought she may be an older female, and this wide, rounded foot shape might be indicative of what an actual sasquatches foot would appear to look like. The Wrinkle Foot prints measure around 14 inches.

Paul and 8-year-old Michael after a Salmon fishing trip in Ilwaco, Washington, 1985.

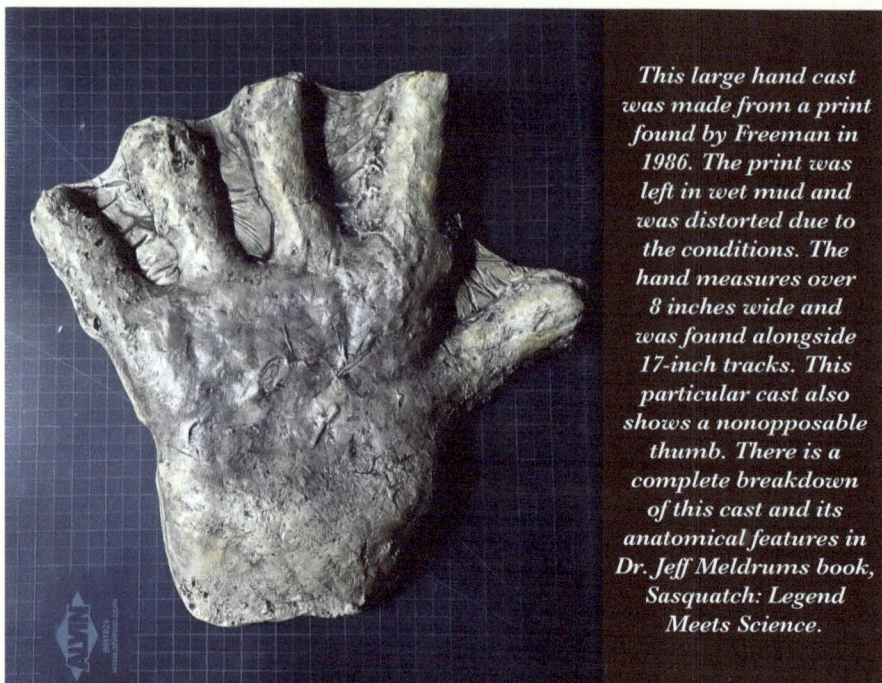

This large hand cast was made from a print found by Freeman in 1986. The print was left in wet mud and was distorted due to the conditions. The hand measures over 8 inches wide and was found alongside 17-inch tracks. This particular cast also shows a nonopposable thumb. There is a complete breakdown of this cast and its anatomical features in Dr. Jeff Meldrums book, Sasquatch: Legend Meets Science.

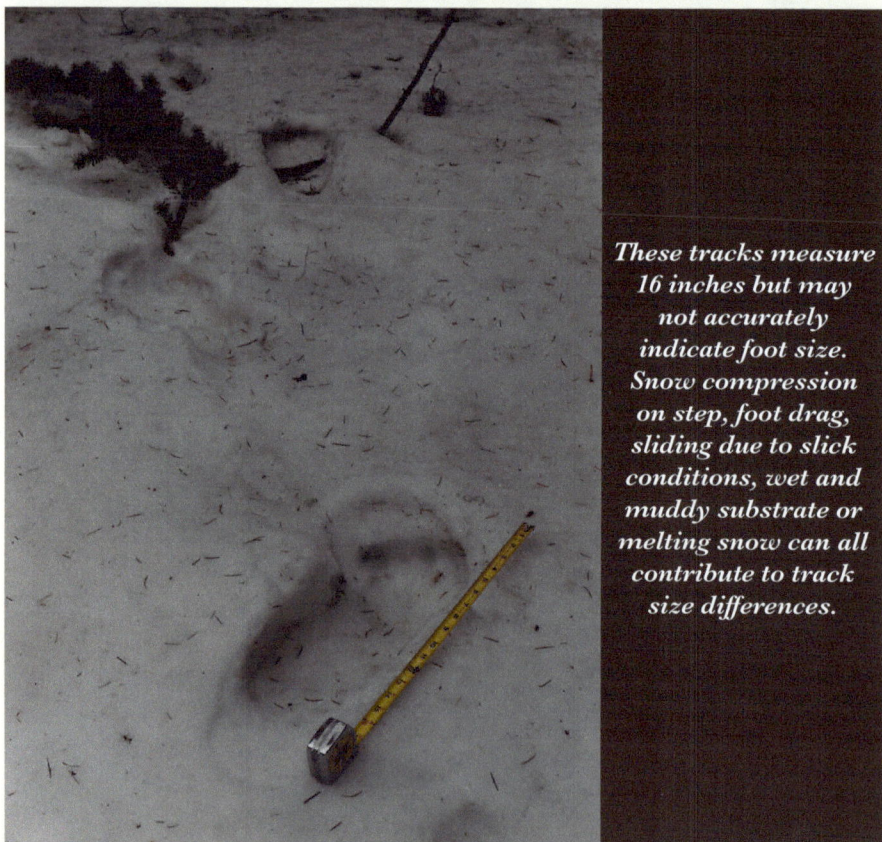

These tracks measure 16 inches but may not accurately indicate foot size. Snow compression on step, foot drag, sliding due to slick conditions, wet and muddy substrate or melting snow can all contribute to track size differences.

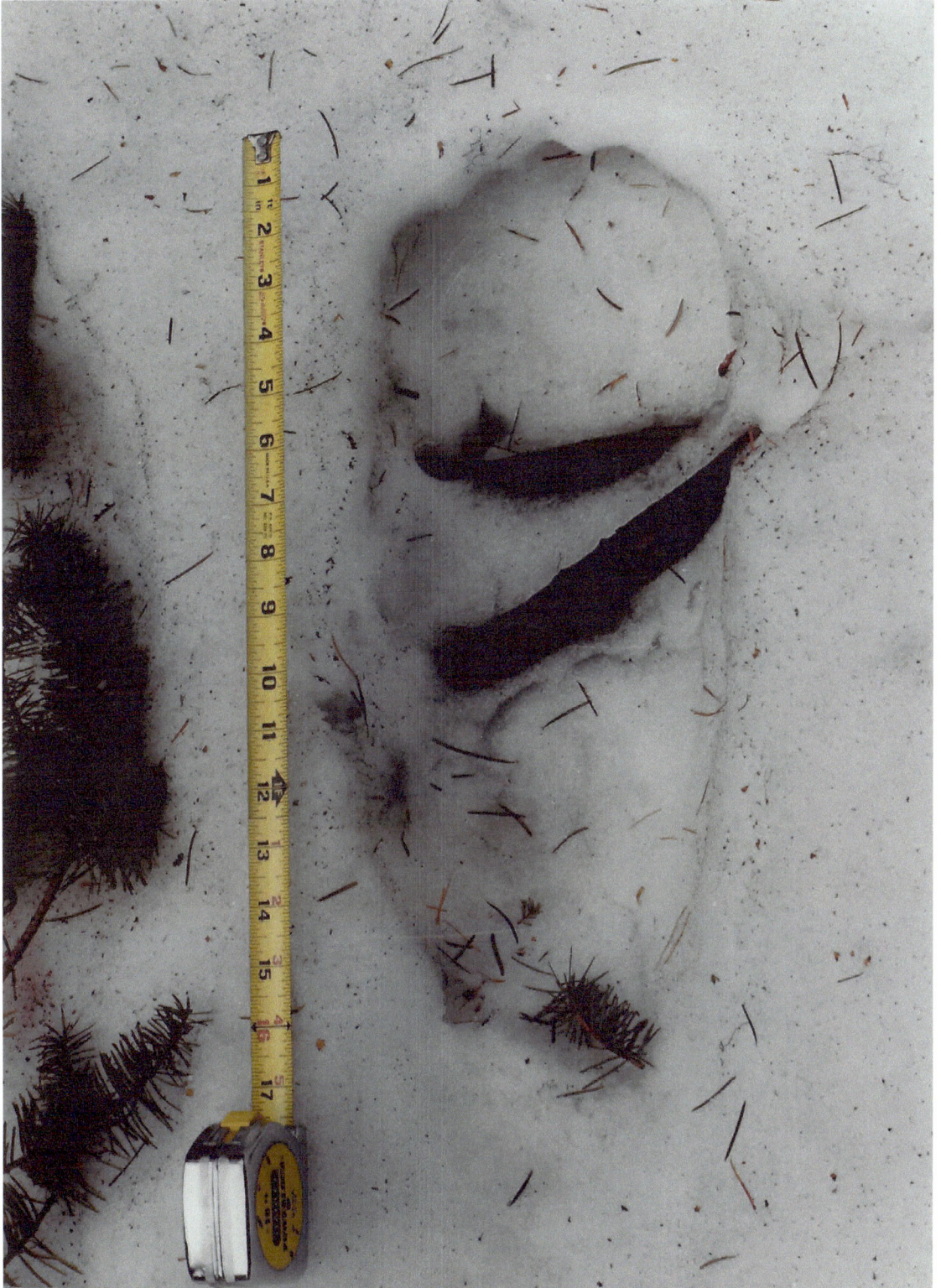

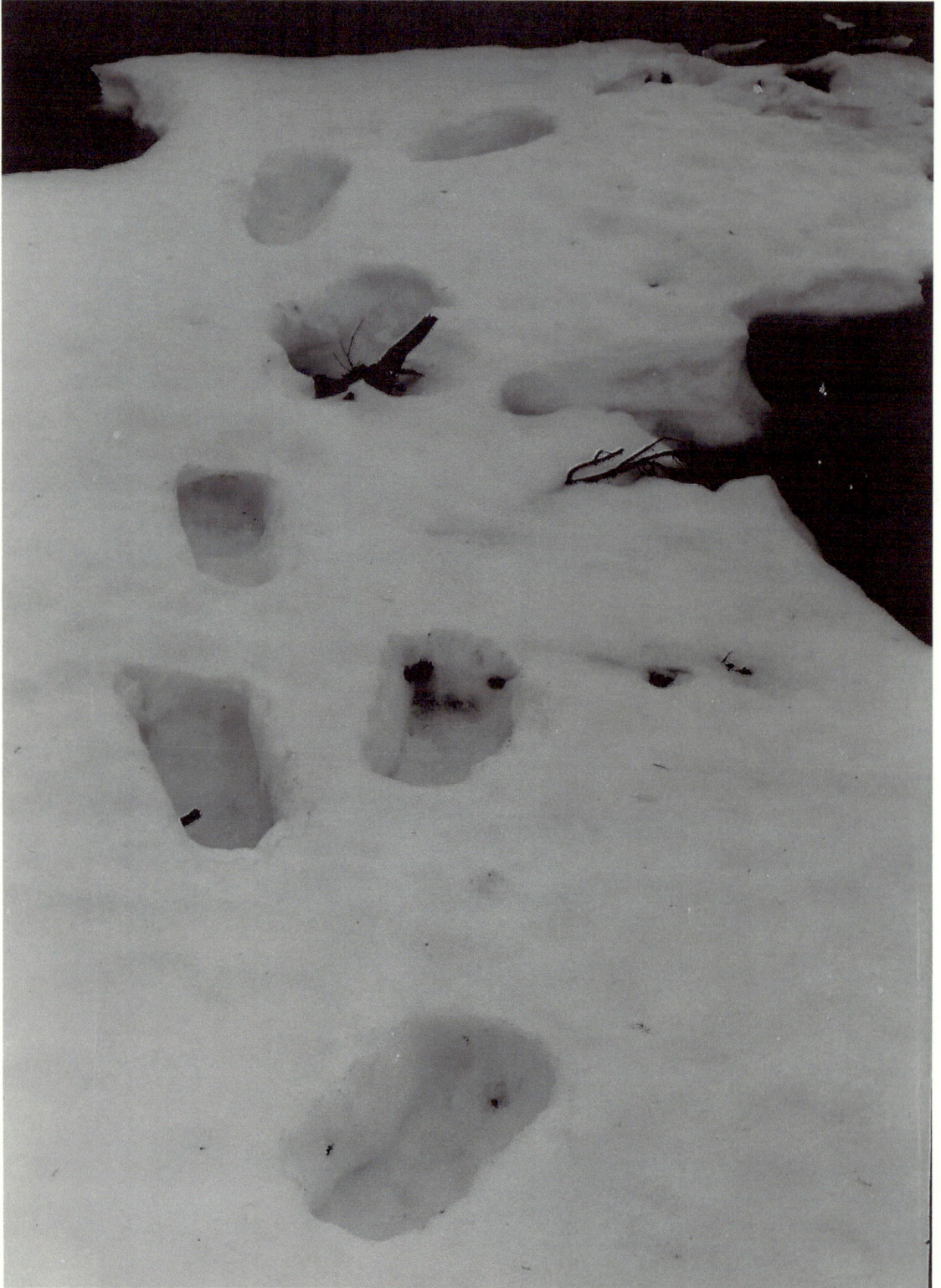

Paul Examines a stripped and broken tree from horseback in 1987.

It was back-breaking work just getting in and out. And in the end, proved to be unsuccessful. The challenge of removing one's body if it had occurred would have been monumental. I suppose he could have cut off a head, or a hand or foot and brought that out. If he made it out that is. He always felt as though he was being watched in there, and if he had shot and killed one, he himself may have been long forgotten by now.

Hunting

In 1987, Good Morning America happened. We had moved back to Walla Walla in the summer of 1986, and I had just turned ten years old when a slick piece of editing, which wasn't even done well, attempted to paint my dad as a hoaxer. I like to refer to it as the hatchet job from hell. As a matter of fact, the whole program was slanted to make my dad along with Wes Sumerlin, and Rene Dahinden look like crazy liars. It was a satirical piece from the start, the two cowboys from Walla Walla, and the little Canuck fell right into the trap. A straight answer to a simple question is all it took to doom my father. When asked if he had ever made fake tracks my dad answered honestly, "Yes I have. I've made tracks in my garden. I've made tracks and tried to cast them to see if a man is capable of doing this." But if you've ever seen this show then you already know that is not what was aired. Instead, a national audience got to hear him simply say, yes I have. That left a black cloud over my dad that still follows him even today. Cliff Barackman and Jeff Meldrum will tell you that any researcher worth his salt has done the same thing. Before you can accept that what you are looking at can be real, you must first eliminate all possibilities of it being not real. Paul Freeman was eliminating possibilities. Good Morning America was eliminating Paul Freeman. I still won't watch that damn show.

Back to The City

Back to Walla Walla

1987 was also the year that a few "super" expeditions took place, and the first time that I, now 10 years old, was taken and exposed to the research. There were a couple of significant trackways found that year in mid-April, and then again on May 9th that drew much interest, and are still being analyzed today. As a result, a number of the who's who in the Bigfoot community came to see these tracks and work with my father. Rene Dahinden was there and had also been there in 82' as well. Bob Titmus and John Green were two others that had been there to study tracks found in 1982 that would come to investigate the 87' tracks, as well as the 1991 Mill Creek Road, tracks nine years later. Grover Krantz was there of course, as he spent a lot of time around my father in those days, and the man supported my father's evidence all the way til' the end. Also present were Peter Byrne and a man named Greg May, a Washington State University Wilderness Survival Instructor and tracker. May, who was also a protege of Krantz's so to speak, would become a familiar face in my dad's entourage for a few years to follow.

As an author's note: I will speak freely and say that it is a tremendous shame that the aforementioned giants of Bigfoot research history, the ones who came to be with my father, ended up turning on one another and eating each other like hungry sharks by the end of their lives. Byrne, of course, being the sole surviving member to this day.

John Green

Their Own Opinion

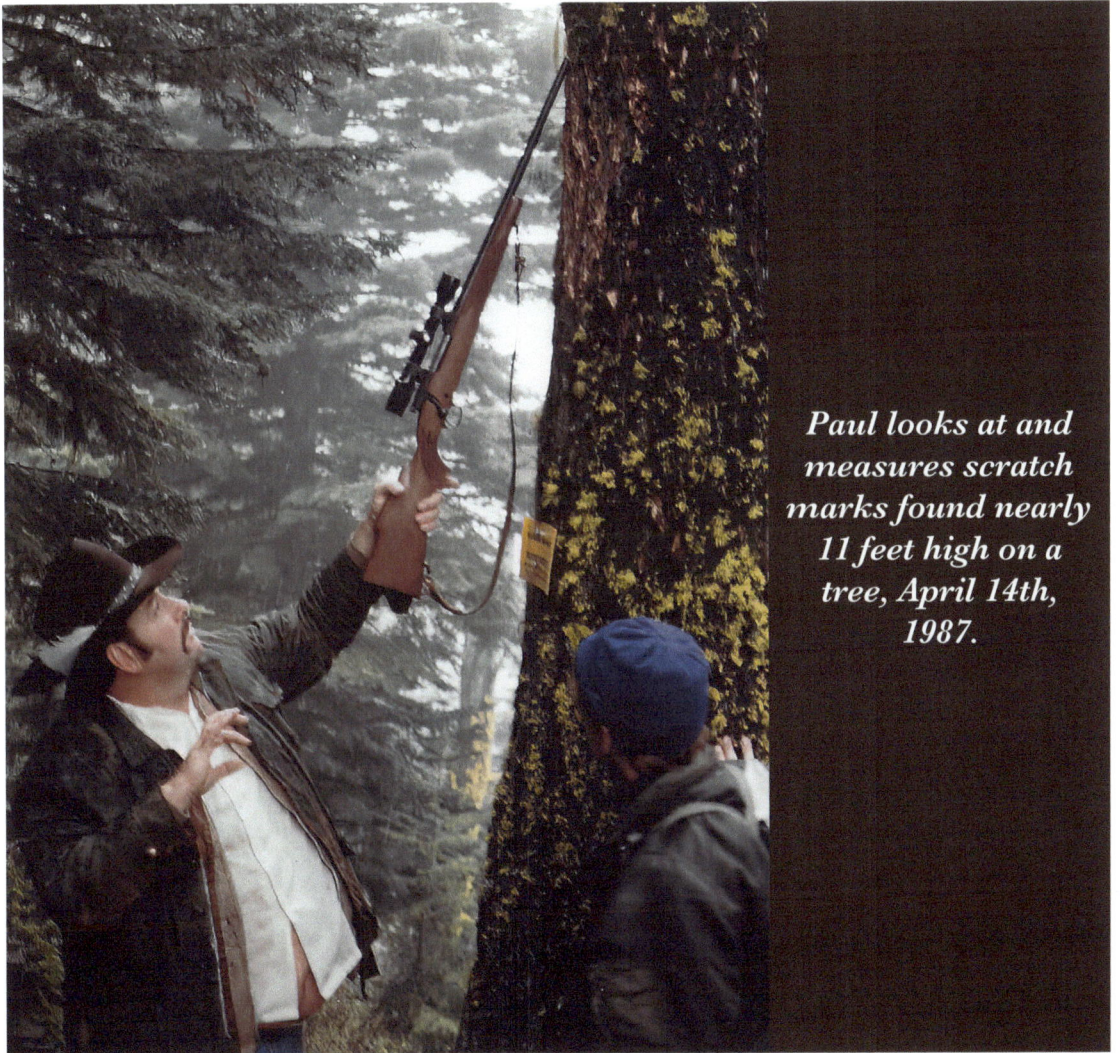

Paul looks at and measures scratch marks found nearly 11 feet high on a tree, April 14th, 1987.

Paul Freeman and Rene Dahinden just below the site of Paul's original encounter. Photo taken Winter, 1987.

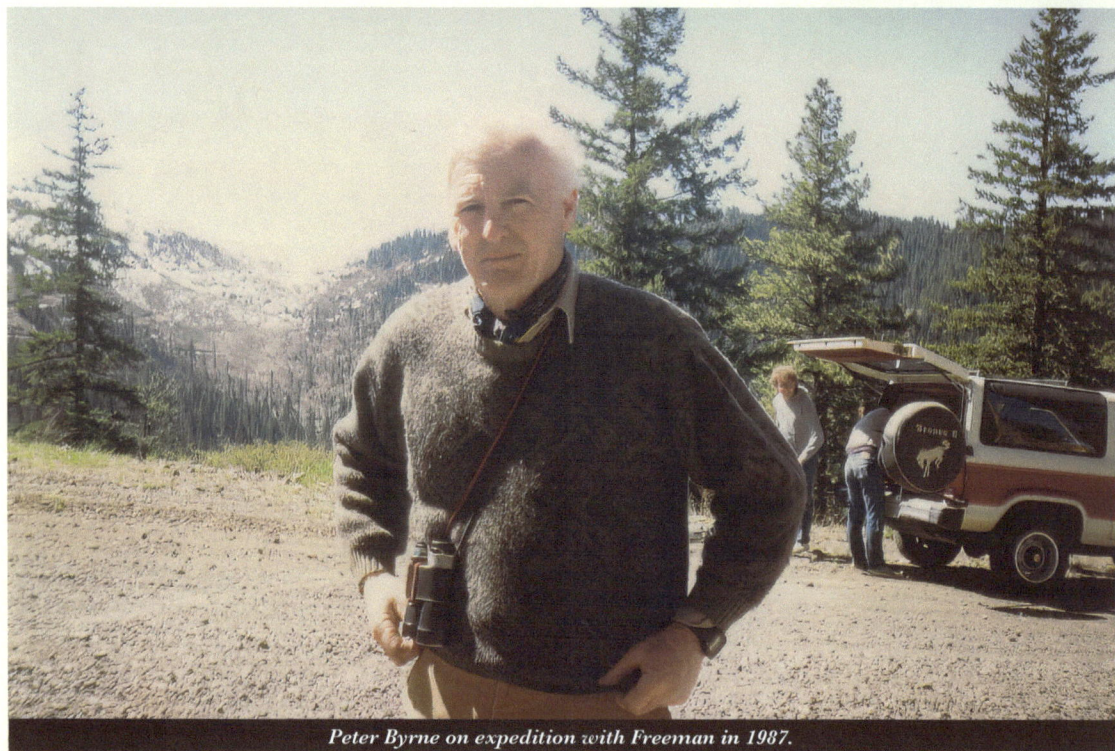

Peter Byrne on expedition with Freeman in 1987.

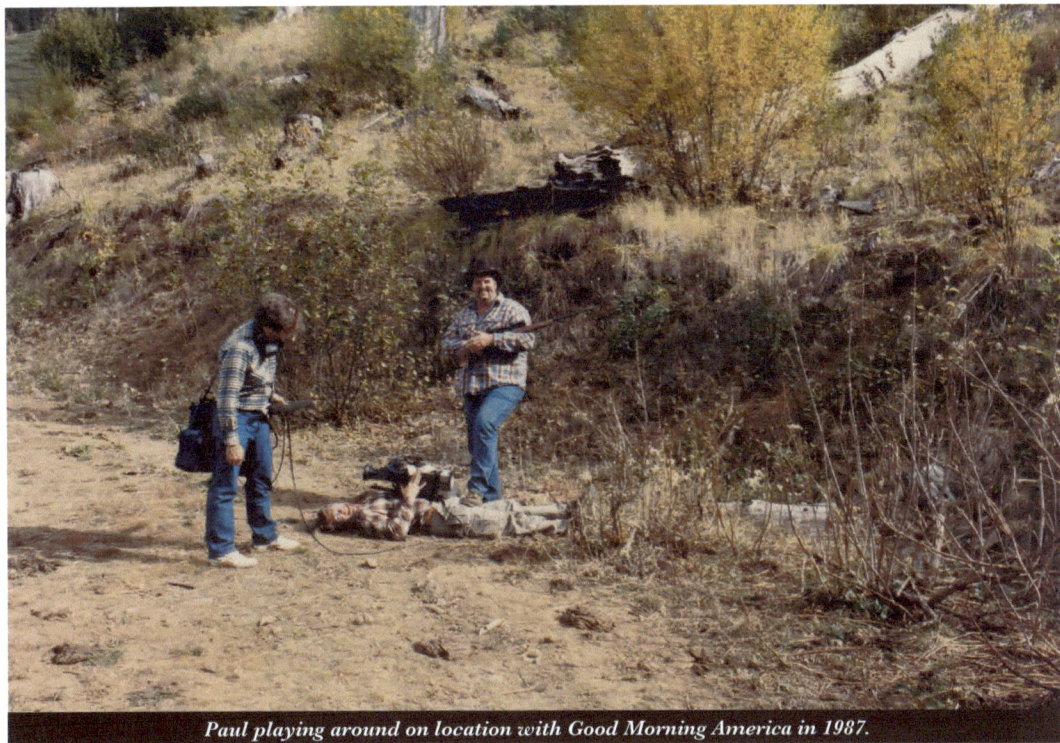

Paul playing around on location with Good Morning America in 1987.

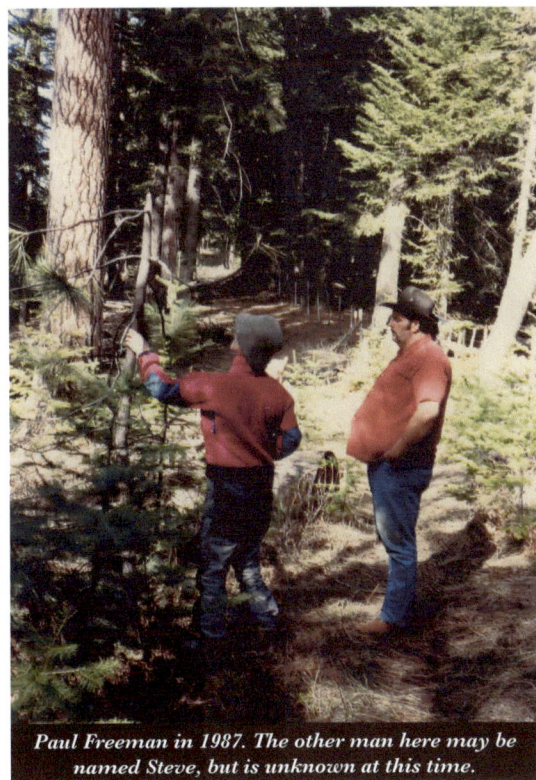

Paul Freeman in 1987. The other man here may be named Steve, but is unknown at this time.

Paul with Jennie Fisher, an elementary student he helped with a school project and even took on a mini-expedition. Photo courtesy of Jennie Fisher-Turner.

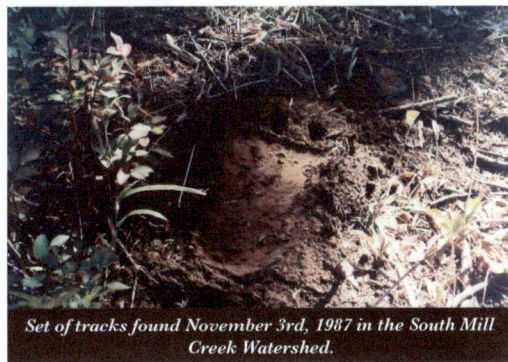

Set of tracks found November 3rd, 1987 in the South Mill Creek Watershed.

Paul pointing out a possible hair sample on a stripped branch, April 14th, 1987.

Set of tracks found November 3rd, 1987 in the South Mill Creek Watershed.

November 3rd, 1987.

Set of tracks found November 3rd, 1987 in the South Mill Creek Watershed.

Bigfoot hunter says he found tracks in the Blues

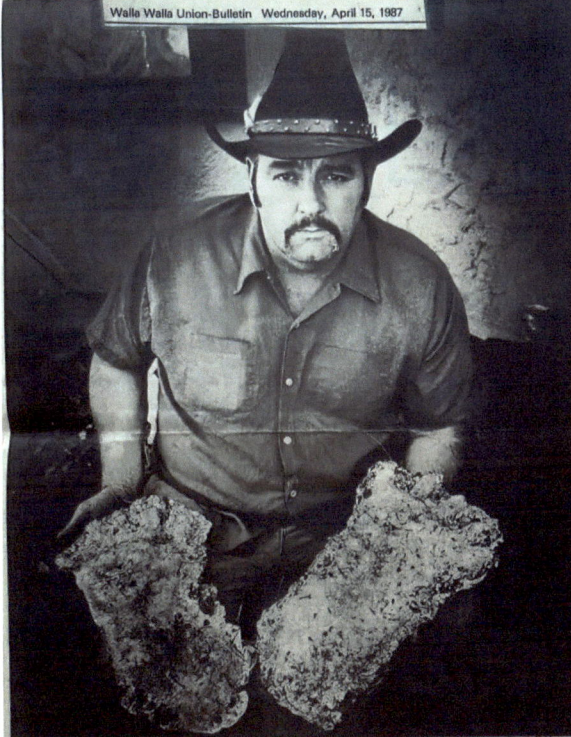

Walla Walla Union-Bulletin Wednesday, April 15, 1987

By TERRY CHURCH
Of the Union-Bulletin

Bigfoot is back in the Blues.

Local Bigfoot hunter Paul Freeman claims the proof is in the prints — the footprints.

"Those guys are really traveling around; they're sure tearing up the ground up there," said Freeman, noting his most recent discovery came Thursday when he found some tracks near Indian Ridge on Tiger Canyon Road in the Blue Mountains.

But Freeman, who claims he finds Bigfoot tracks annually in this area, said this time he also found hair samples from the beast.

"The important thing is the hair samples," said Freeman, adding the footprints ran ¾ of a mile, about 20 miles southeast of here.

Freeman, a 44-year-old former Mill Creek Watershed patrol rider with the U.S. Forest Service, reported spotting an 8-foot-tall animal covered with reddish-black hair in June 1982. Later that month he quit his job, citing "a lot of hassle and pressure over the Bigfoot thing, both from the public and the forest service."

He claimed his discovery last week was in nearly the same area where he spotted the creature in 1982.

After his recent finding he immediately called Grover Krantz, a Washington State University physical anthropologist, who came to Walla Walla Saturday to make plaster casts of footprints and gather hair samples.

"These are some of the better ones I've seen," said Krantz in a telephone interview this morning. "I would call it a fairly important finding."

Krantz said he is "reasonably sure" the hair samples — only the second time such samples have been found — are authentic.

Krantz is adamant about his view of Bigfoot.

"It is not strong enough to say I 'believe' there is (a Bigfoot). I have seen evidence that cannot be explained any other way," he said.

In fact, Krantz said footprints found show there have been as many as four of the beasts in this area. Krantz said he sells exact copies of plaster casts through WSU, but the money made doesn't even meet costs of making the copies.

Freeman took pictures of the footprints found last week and made casts of his own. One measured nearly 17 inches long and 9 inches wide, he said.

And after Krantz's arrival came two people representing a Pullman-based group called "Bigfoot Expedition 1."

GREG MAY

"We're the only scientifically-based organization working on discovery of the animal," said 28-year-old Greg May, director of the group.

"This is important in the fact that one of the prints found is the same individual that Mr. Freeman sighted in 1982," said May, who works with Krantz in the pursuit of Bigfoot, also known as Sasquatch.

May said he hopes if Bigfoot is involved in some type of vehicle-animal accident that his group can attain control of the body.

"We want to deal with it respectfully and with some semblance of class," he said. "We want to eliminate any circus atmosphere."

Freeman said he currently works about seven months of the year in harvest jobs, but his main goal is to find Bigfoot.

He conceded that his belief in the beast has made him the subject of ridicule.

"I just don't pay any attention to it anymore," he said.

He said it's going to take the body of the animal to convince non-believers.

"It's a shame to have to kill one, but I think that is the only way to convince people of its existence."

U-B photo by Jeff Horner

Bigfoot hunter Paul Freeman shows plaster casts made from his discovery of footprints in the Blue Mountains last week. Freeman said one of the tracks measured nearly 17 inches long and 9 inches wide. Greg May, pictured at right, from the Pullman-based "Bigfoot Expedition 1," came to Walla Walla after hearing about the footprints found by Freeman.

An article from the Walla Walla Union Bulletin April 15, 1987.

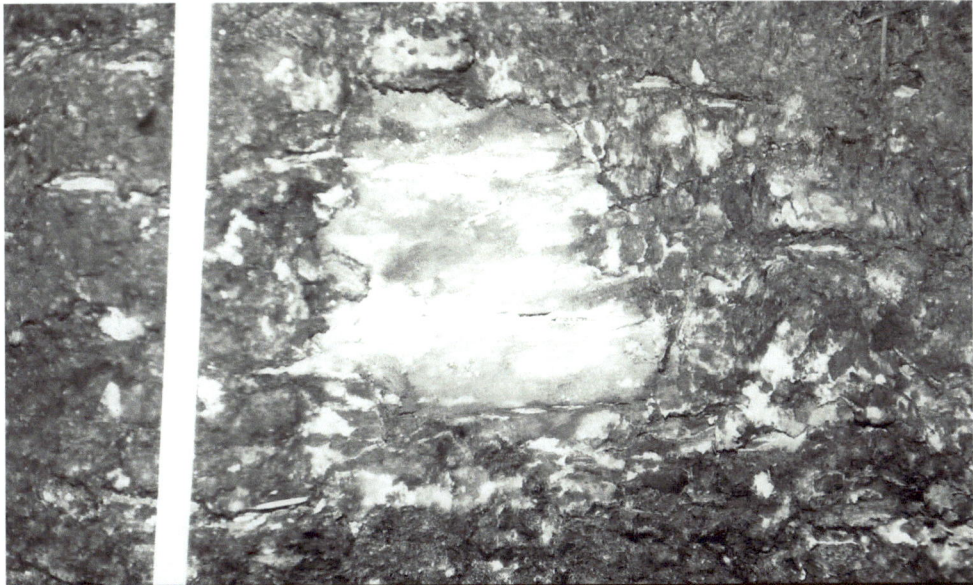

A cast being made of south watershed tracks found November 3rd, 1987.

Southeast watershed May 9th, 1987.

Another print from the May 9th, 1987 trackway.

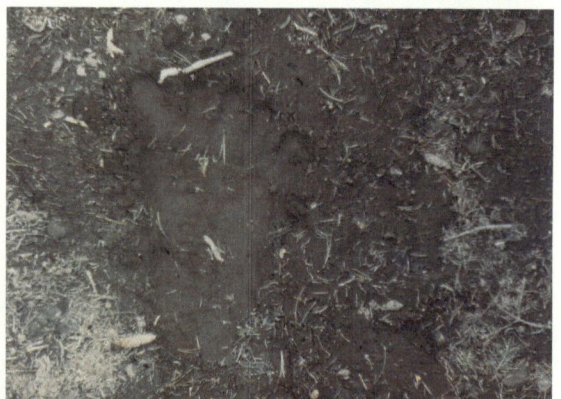

Close up of right footprint from southeast watershed May 9th, 1987.

The trackway leading into the snow from May 9th, 1987.

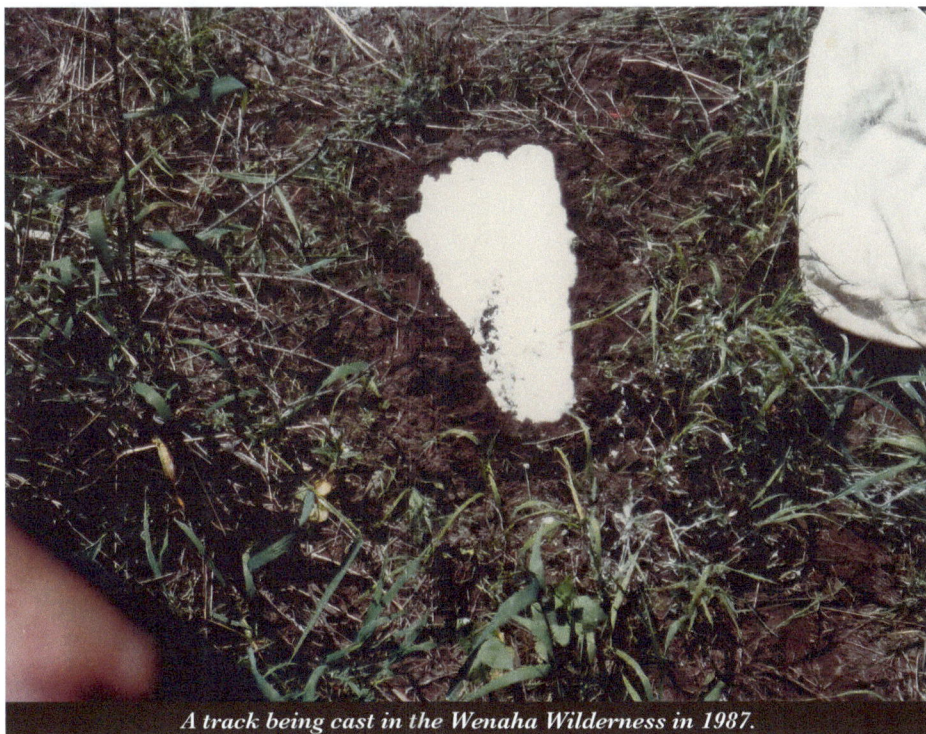

A track being cast in the Wenaha Wilderness in 1987.

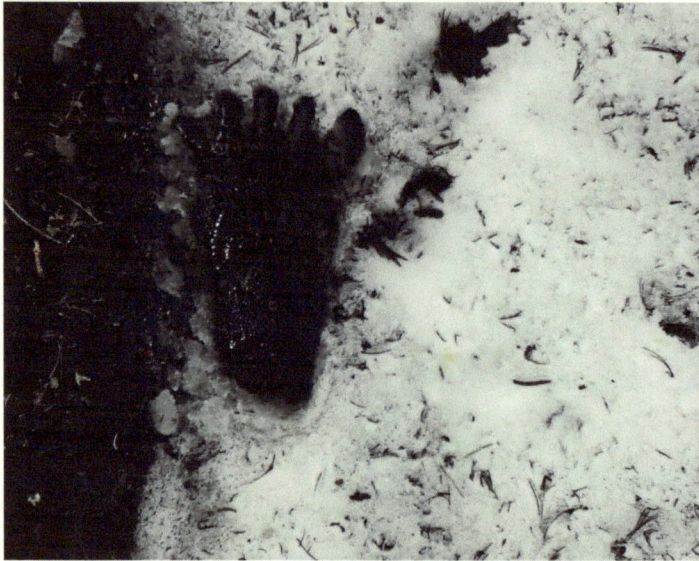

These tracks were thought to be only two to three hours old when found near the southeast watershed on May 9th, 1987 and drew great interest from known researchers. There is no doubt as to what individual these tracks belong to. Look at the unique pinky toe placement and the almost "squared off" big toe. These tracks belong to Wrinkle Foot.

Paul with Wes Sumerlin behind him examining possible scratch marks at May 9th,1987 trackway.

*Scientific Education System
By Redken*

TO: Cindy Hyland, SES CONSULTANT # 322
FROM: Clara Patterson-Hicks
DATE: December 4, 1987
SUBJECT: BIG FOOT HAIR SAMPLES: PROPERTY OF PAUL FREEMAN

Dear Cindy:

Sorry to have taken so long in getting around to looking at
"ole Big Foot's" hair, but I've been travelling a lot for
Redken and have not been in the office very much since the 1st
of August.

The hair is different from any I've ever looked at in my 25
years of hair analization. Since I do not have a "Big Foot"
comparison and as you advised - he isn't available for interview,
all I can tell you is that it IS hair, but is not completely
human or animal. I've never seen hair of this nature! Most of
the hair fibers were fractured as in photo # 1. Also note the
even, almost fluid like appearance of the medullary canal in
photo # 2. The green retardation color is also something I've
never seen. All human or animal hair will retard yellow and
magenta regardless of condition. All the hairs I looked at(20)
were this shade of green.

The only other possibility is that the hair was human and a
chemical process was applied then dyed with a very strong chemical
before being made into a wig. But again, I have looked at lots of
wig hair through the years and this shade of green has never been
seen by me and when hair is chemically processed for wig making,
the medulla is completely destroyed or diffused in the process.
This hair still has a very different medullary structure ????

The mystery still lives.

Kara

HP/js

*Results of testing conducted on a hair sample collected at the North Fork of the Walla Walla River by
Paul Freeman in 1987.*

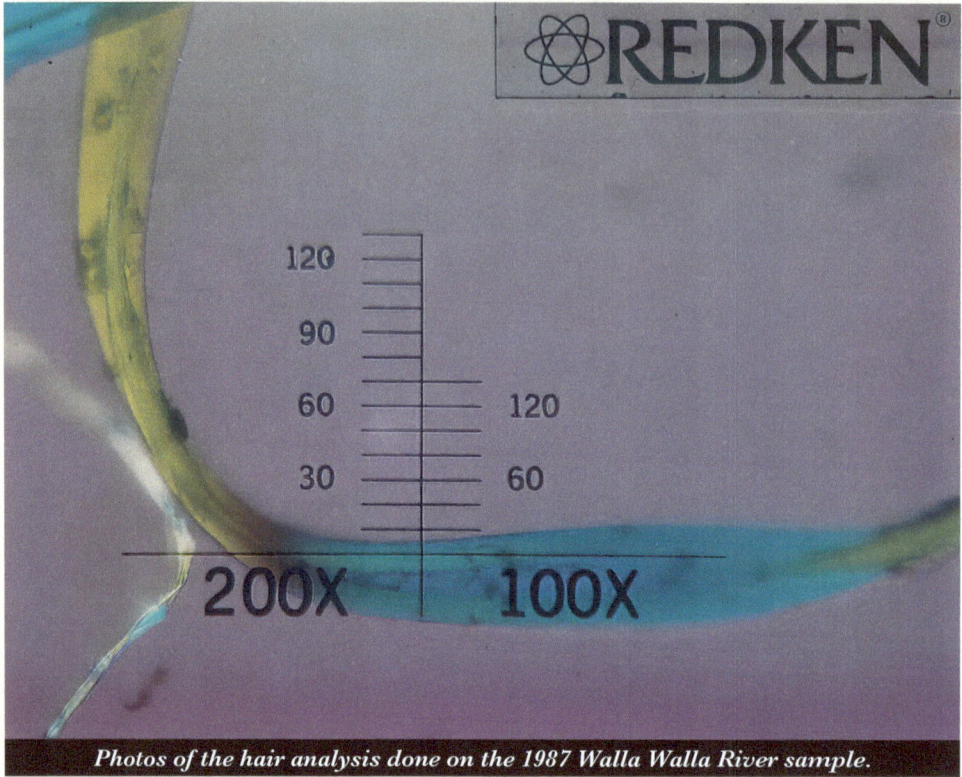

Photos of the hair analysis done on the 1987 Walla Walla River sample.

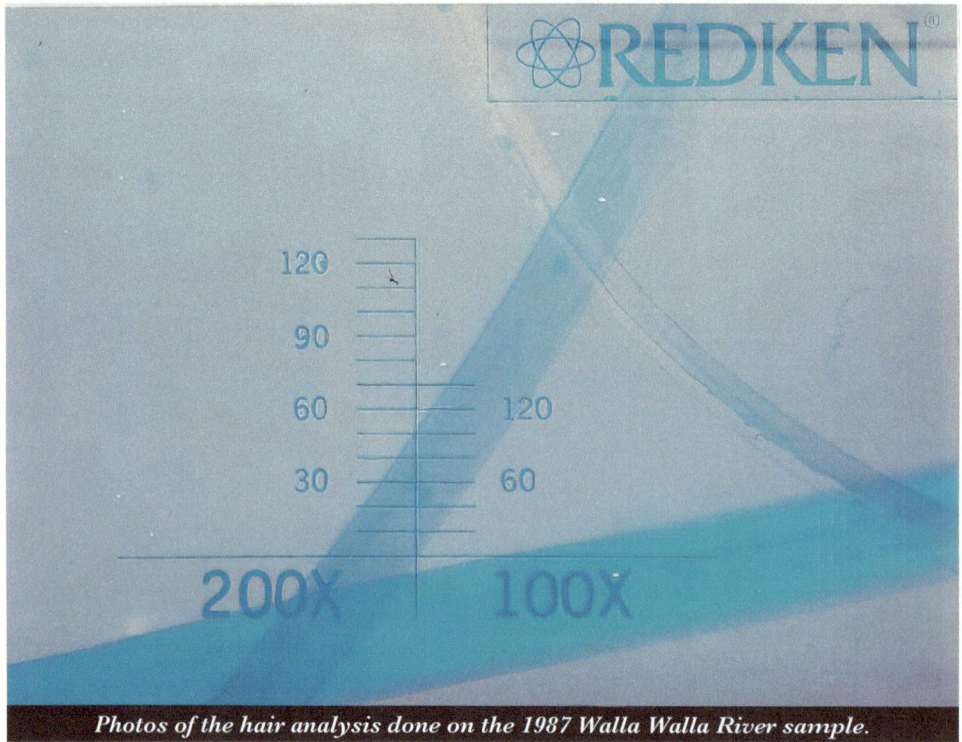

Photos of the hair analysis done on the 1987 Walla Walla River sample.

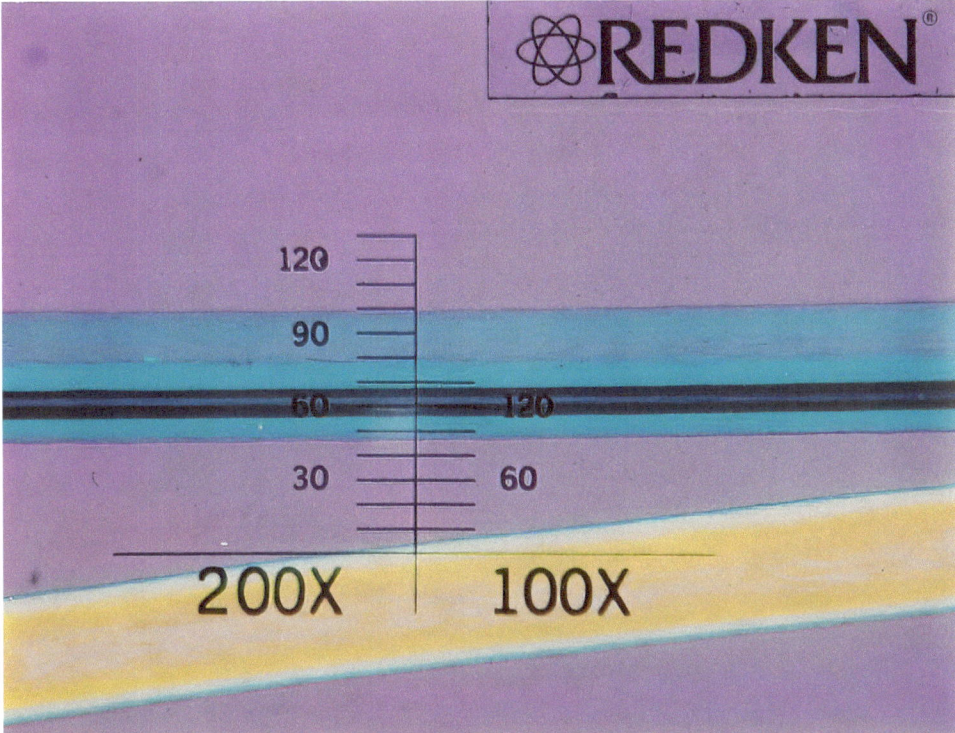

Photos of the hair analysis done on the 1987 Walla Walla River sample.

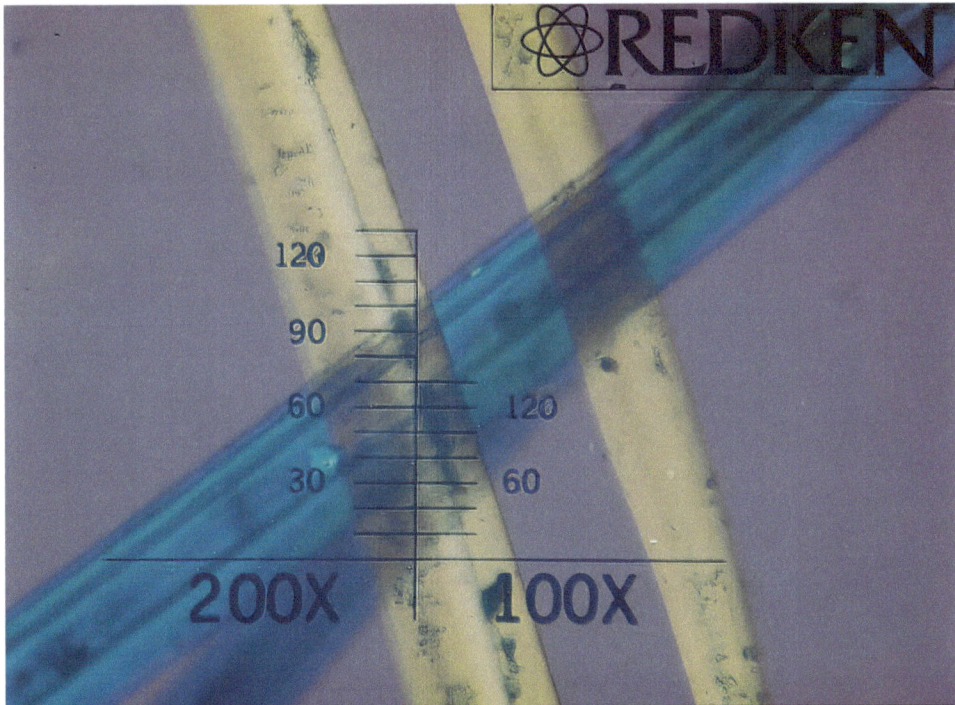

Photos of the hair analysis done on the 1987 Walla Walla River sample.

Paul and Duane Freeman give a tour of the mountains to the crew of Good Morning America in 1987.

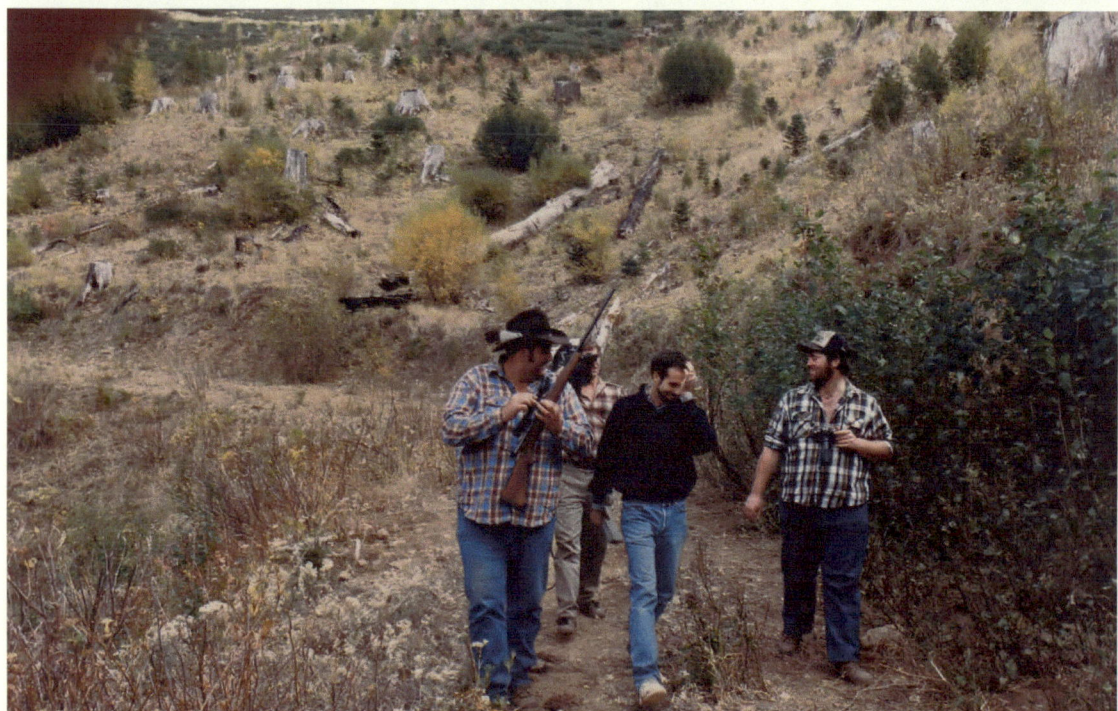

Paul, Duane, and the man from New York with the busted eye tour the site of Paul's original encounter in 1982.

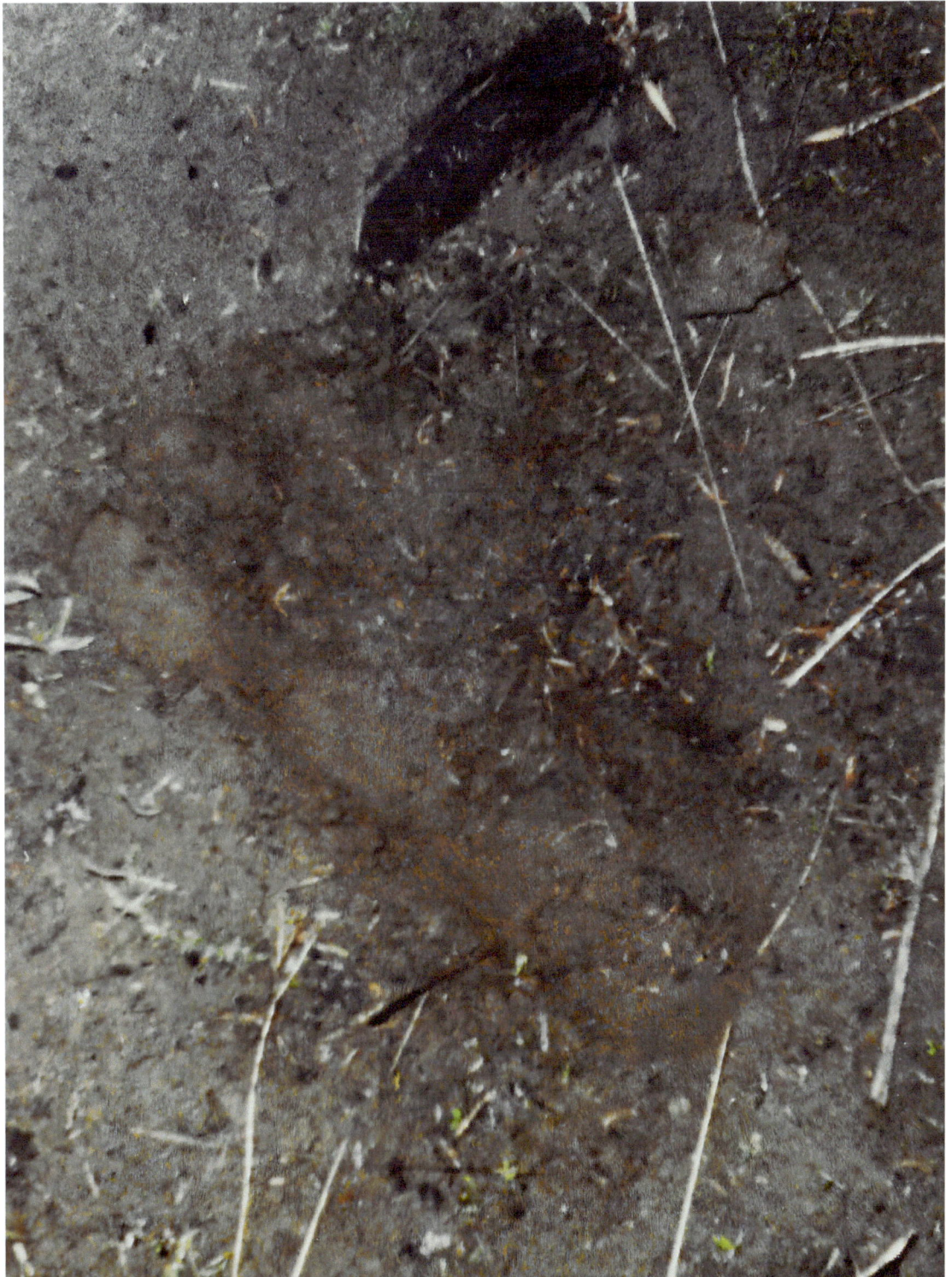

Track found June of 1987.

Northside Mill Creek Watershed April 28th, 1987, these tracks would measure in at 16-17 inches and are believed to be of the elusive male in the area.

Northside watershed April 28th, 1987.

Freeman examining a broken tree branch in the Blue Mountains May 14th, 1987.

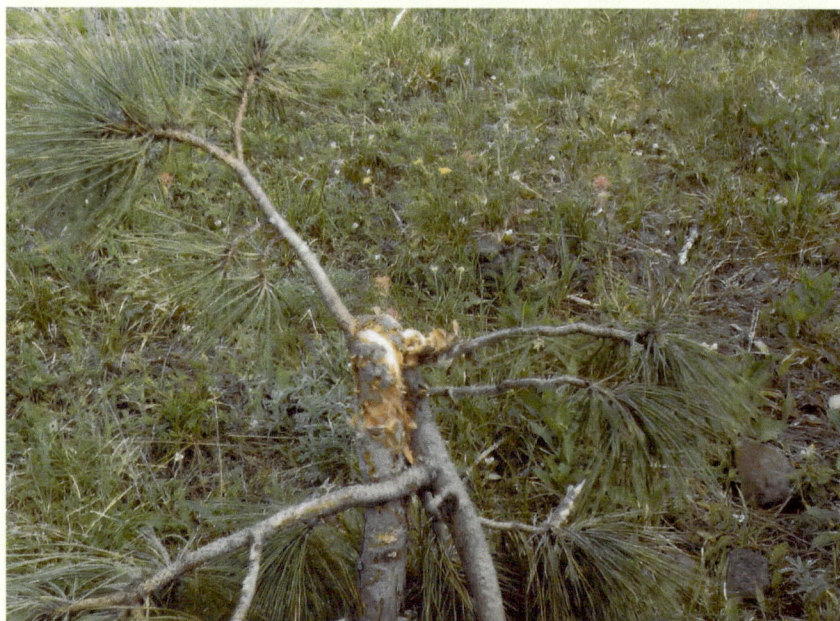

Broken, twisted branches can be a sign of Bigfoot, and may contain collectible hair samples.

Bigfoot hunter says he found

tracks in the Blues

By TERRY CHURCH
Of the Union-Bulletin

Bigfoot is back in the Blues.

Local Bigfoot hunter Paul Freeman claims the proof is in the prints — the footprints.

"Those guys are really traveling around; they're sure tearing up the ground up there," said Freeman, noting his most recent discovery came Thursday when he found some tracks near Indian Ridge on Tiger Canyon Road in the Blue Mountains.

But Freeman, who claims he finds Bigfoot tracks annually in this area, said this time he also found hair samples from the beast.

"The important thing is the hair samples," said Freeman, adding the footprints ran ¾ of a mile, about 20 miles southeast of here.

Freeman, a 44-year-old former Mill Creek Watershed patrol rider with the U.S. Forest Service, reported spotting an 8-foot-tall animal covered with reddish-black hair in June 1982. Later that month he quit his job, citing "a lot of hassle and pressure over the Bigfoot thing, both from the public and the forest service."

He claimed his discovery last week was in nearly the same area where he spotted the creature in 1982.

After his recent finding he immediately called Grover Krantz, a Washington State University physical anthropologist, who came to Walla Walla Saturday to make plaster casts of footprints and gather hair samples.

"These are some of the better ones I've seen," said Krantz in a telephone interview this morning. "I would call it a fairly important finding."

Krantz said he is "reasonably sure" the hair samples — only the second time such samples have been found — are authentic.

Krantz is adamant about his view of Bigfoot.

"It is not strong enough to say I 'believe' there is (a Bigfoot). I have seen evidence that cannot be explained any other way," he said.

In fact, Krantz said footprints found show there have been as many as four of the beasts in this area. Krantz said he sells exact copies of plaster casts through WSU, but the money made doesn't even meet costs of making the copies.

Freeman took pictures of the footprints found last week and made casts of his own. One measured nearly 17 inches long and 9 inches wide, he said.

And after Krantz's arrival came two people representing a Pullman-based group called "Bigfoot Expedition 1."

"We're the only scientifically-based organization working on discovery of the animal," said 28-year-old Greg May, director of the group.

"This is important in the fact that one of the prints found is the same individual that Mr. Freeman sighted in 1982," said May, who works with Krantz in the pursuit of Bigfoot, also known as Sasquatch.

May said he hopes if Bigfoot is involved in some type of vehicle-animal accident that his group can attain control of the body.

"We want to deal with it respectfully and with some semblance of class," he said. "We want to eliminate any circus atmosphere."

Freeman said he currently works about seven months of the year in harvest jobs, but his main goal is to find Bigfoot.

He conceded that his belief in the beast has made him the subject of ridicule.

"I just don't pay any attention to it anymore," he said.

He said it's going to take the body of the animal to convince non-believers.

"It's a shame to have to kill one, but I think that is the only way to convince people of its existence."

An article written for the Union Bulletin about a recent track and hair sample find. 1987.

These branches, twisted as well as broken, are all but impossible for a man to do himself.

These tracks were found in September of 1987 and show where this animal crossed a road.

You can see where this print was nearly driven over before being discovered.

Green pools and sunlit foam spar-
kling cascades and luxuriant foliage
moon-rock gorges blue grey morn-
ings white sand bars camp fire
companionship otters and dolphins
eagles and kingfishers warm
weather, blue skies
jungle camps wildlife
seminars all on a
river expedition
in the pristine,
unspoiled
wilderness
of the NW
mountains
of the
kingdom
of Nepal
with:

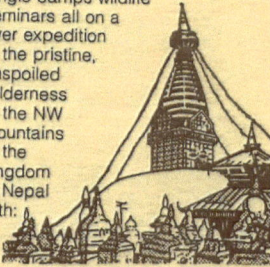

Peter Byrne

Expeditions, Inc.

Dear Paul:

Just a quick note to thank you for
letting me join you on the recent
outing in eastern Oregon.

I was in NY recently and saw some
of the Channell Five people there
and asked them for the tape. They
have promised to send me a copy and
if I get one then I will make a copy
and send it to you.

All good wishes and thanks again and
when you see Grover give him my regards
and tell him that I would like to meet
with him one of these days.

Best wishes,

Peter Byrne.

A letter from Peter Byrne to Paul in 1987.

Bob Titmus examining a broken tree branch in May of 1987.

Grover Krantz can be seen looking at marks on a tree with Wes Sumerlin as Paul prepares to mix plaster to cast a track in 1987.

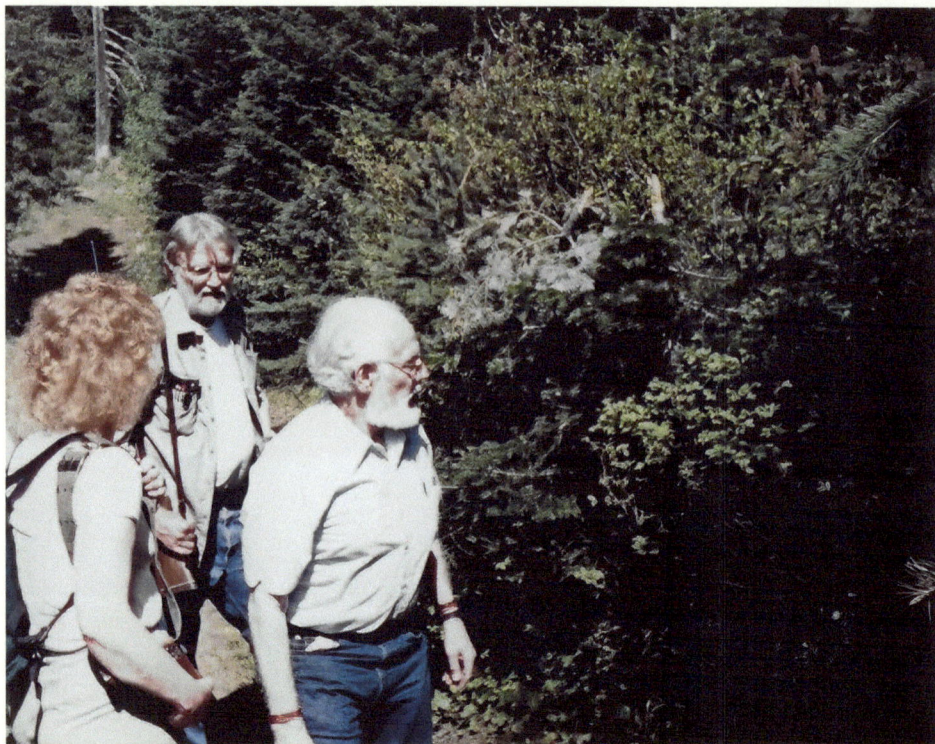

Grover Krantz and Bob Titmus in May of 1987.

Bill Laughery measuring a recent trackway. Date and location unknown.

Paul Freeman and Greg May compare thoughts on a set of tracks in May 1987.

A footprint was examined in 1987. This is the man I believe to be named Steve.

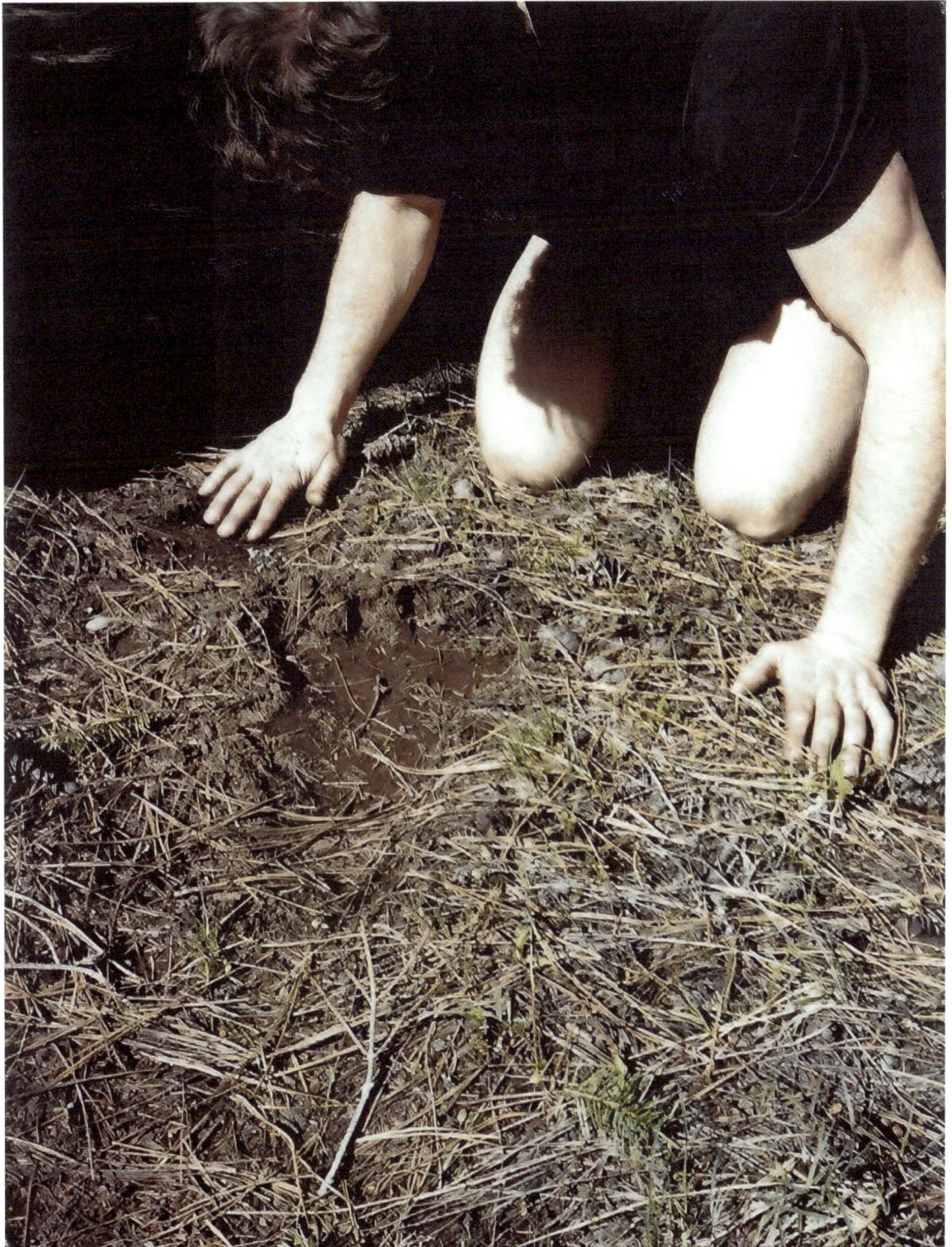

Washington State University Survival Instructor Greg May examines a track in the Blue Mountains in 1987.

Track found at Bear Trap Springs in September of 1988.

July 1988 location unknown.

This photo, taken in the Wenaha Wilderness in 1988 shows plaster drying in the track to form what will be a cast of that footprint.

Indian Ridge
April 15TH 1987
~~Found in Bed~~

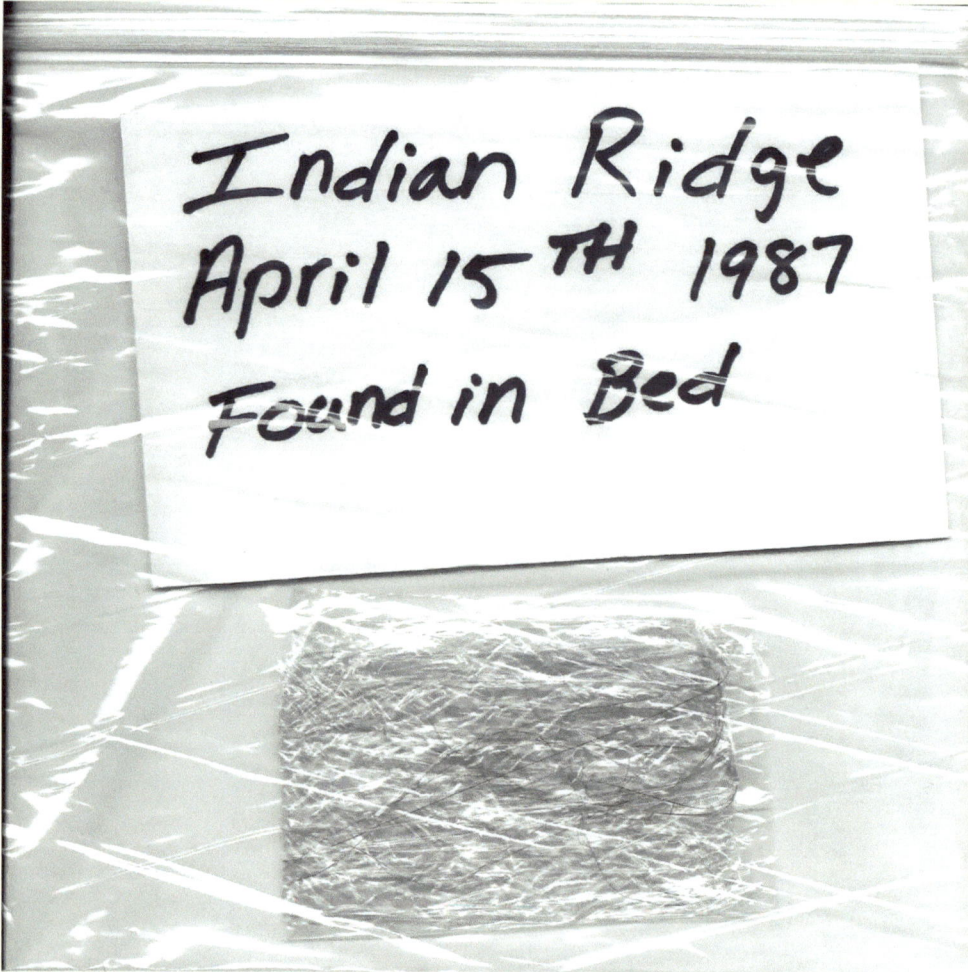

A hair sample collected from a possible bed at Indian Ridge in the Blue Mountains on April 15, 1987.

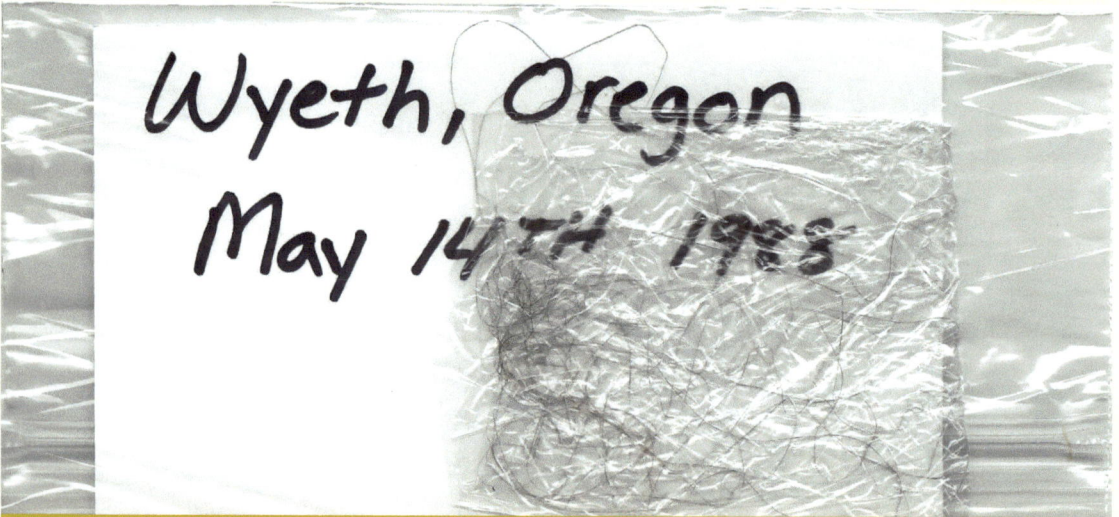

Wyeth, Oregon
May 14TH 1988

Hair sample collected in Wyeth, Oregon May 14, 1988.

Something I'm often asked is if I've ever seen one, a Bigfoot that is. The answer is no, I've never seen one, and I often think that maybe that's a good thing. I saw the obsession it set off in my father, and I lived with it for fifteen years. And so the answer is, with a sigh of relief, no. But I will tell you the story of the one time that I maybe came close. When I was twelve years old my dad took me with him to go mushroom hunting. I believe Morels were the prize that day, and we were at a place called Green Peak, right outside of Walla Walla Washington, in the Blues. It was overcast that day and we had started down an old trail. We had been on the hunt for maybe twenty minutes when it started to rain. Not a drizzle, but a heavy rain mind you. My dad had decided we should head back, have our sandwich lunch in the truck and wait it out.

The walking wasn't easy as it had started to get slick, and I remember my shoes were getting muddy. As we made our way back we came past an old growth stump on the side of the trail when my dad stopped dead in his tracks, put his finger to his lips to signal me to be quiet, and pointed to the edge of the trail. Right there in front of us, where we had just passed no more than ten minutes prior was a fresh print. So fresh that even in the heavy rainfall it had not yet begun to show signs of filling with water. This was not a bear track. It was unmistakable what it was. This was a Bigfoot track. It had stepped across the trail from one edge to the other and had done so right behind us, within minutes of our passing.

My dad grabbed my arm and we double-timed it back to his old truck. When we got inside he had me lock my door and he pulled his Norma Magnum rifle out of the rack in the back window and laid it across his lap. I remember him telling me to keep my eyes open and that we were probably being watched. I don't know how long we sat there, but when we left he drove me straight home. He then went to get Vance Orchard and Wes Sumerlin. That was 1989, I was twelve years old, and maybe it's a good thing we didn't see one that day. It saw us, I'm sure of that, and that alone scared me. I still get goosebumps talking about it.

It wasn't that common that I was actually out with my dad in the field during any Bigfoot-related activity when I was really young. Rather you want to call it being on expedition, or just plain old Bigfooting, it was something I wasn't exposed to, and I wasn't taken to my first trackway until I was about ten years old. I was aware of what was happening. I heard the talk, I saw the news stories, and I met his friends and research associates. And then there were the casts. There was an entire garage full of Bigfoot evidence, and as a small child, it was an awesome and awe-inspiring place to be. Look, but don't touch was always the rule, but any questions were always answered directly. If I asked, I would get to hold a footprint cast or measure my own hand against one of a giant. I'm not completely certain as to why I was not included until I was older, maybe my dad didn't want to expose me to the dangers that could come from potentially running across a Sasquatch with your five-year-old child in tow. Maybe he didn't want to take the chance of that child becoming curious and attempting to make mud pies in a set of fresh tracks. But as I look back I realize that my father was correct, that was no place for a child to be.

There of course did come a time when I was allowed and included. I was able to listen and to learn. I spent my fair share of time next to my dad in the Blue Mountains, and I can tell you this: there is nothing quite as eerie as coming across a fresh set of tracks and walking into a forest that has stopped like an unwound clock. Not a single chirp of a bird, not the buzz of a bug, nothing but the sound of your own breath. Almost as if the forest itself is holding a truly deep and beautiful secret, and it will tell no tales.

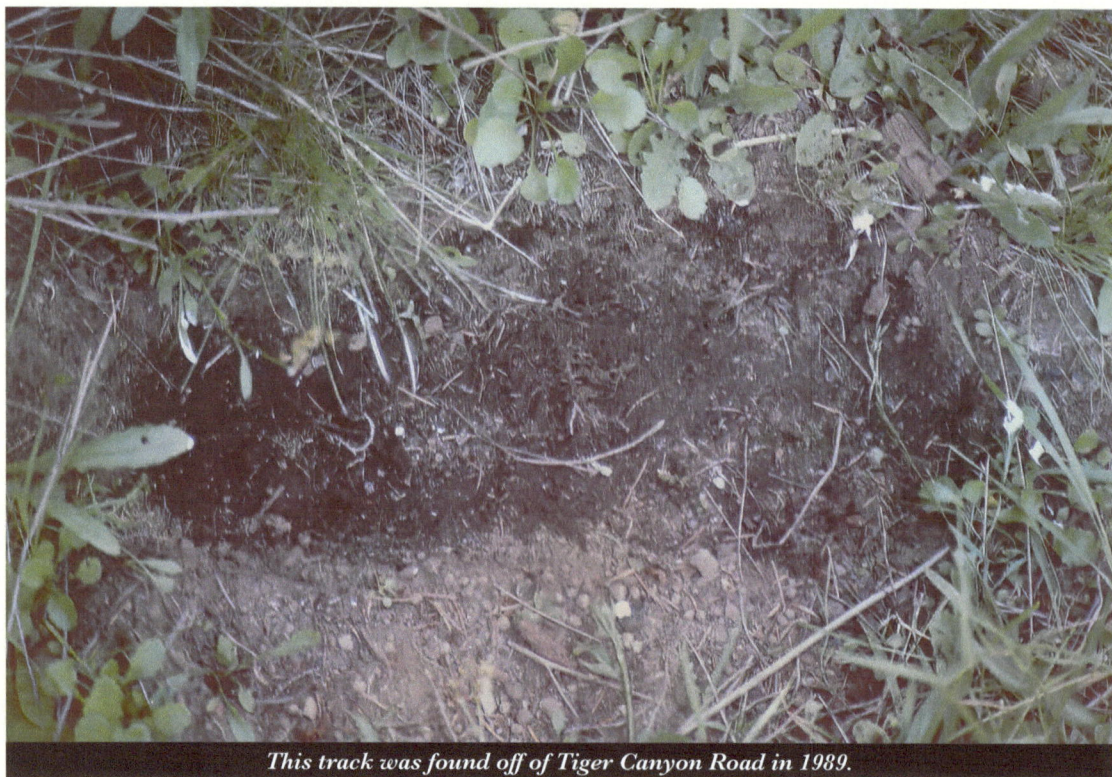

This track was found off of Tiger Canyon Road in 1989.

Another track from 1989. This one was found in the North Watershed area. This is another example of a track showing a wide toe splay that is indicative of the flexibility of the sasquatch foot, and a common trait among numerous prints found by Freeman in the area.

Tracks found on May 8th, 1990.

Paul measuring a track found on May 8th, 1990.

May 8th, 1990.

Monday, January 14th, 1991 was an ordinary day that would lead to what my father would call the "doggonest thing I've seen". My mother and father were having coffee at a local truck stop in Walla Walla that morning when my dad thought he overheard a couple of gentlemen talking about bear tracks. My father was intrigued enough that he decided to go have a look. Together with Vance Orchard and Wes Sumerlin, they made their way to the location to see if there were indeed bear tracks. Instead, they ended up following a set of Bigfoot tracks for nearly two miles. Vance Orchard would later recall Wes Sumerlin immediately recognizing the thirteen-and-a-half-inch tracks, as he could tell that they were made by an old friend of his he affectionately referred to as "Big Jim".

Wes had been finding this animal's tracks for years, and they would continue to be found for years to come. Often referred to as the "7 Mile Tracks", survival instructor Greg May would follow and document the trackway for what would actually be closer to eight miles of solid unbroken tracks. These tracks are highly documented and were cast by numerous individuals that came to the site. I was taken to these tracks by my dad a few days after their discovery, and it was the first time I was allowed to mix plaster for casting. My dad would say that they tracked, and then backtracked again for a total of maybe fifteen miles altogether and that he estimated more than five thousand sets of footprints. This individual creature's tracks would be found again near the same location in 1996, and those would be the tracks that my dad would take Jeff Meldrum to upon their first meeting.

1991 Mill Creek Rd.

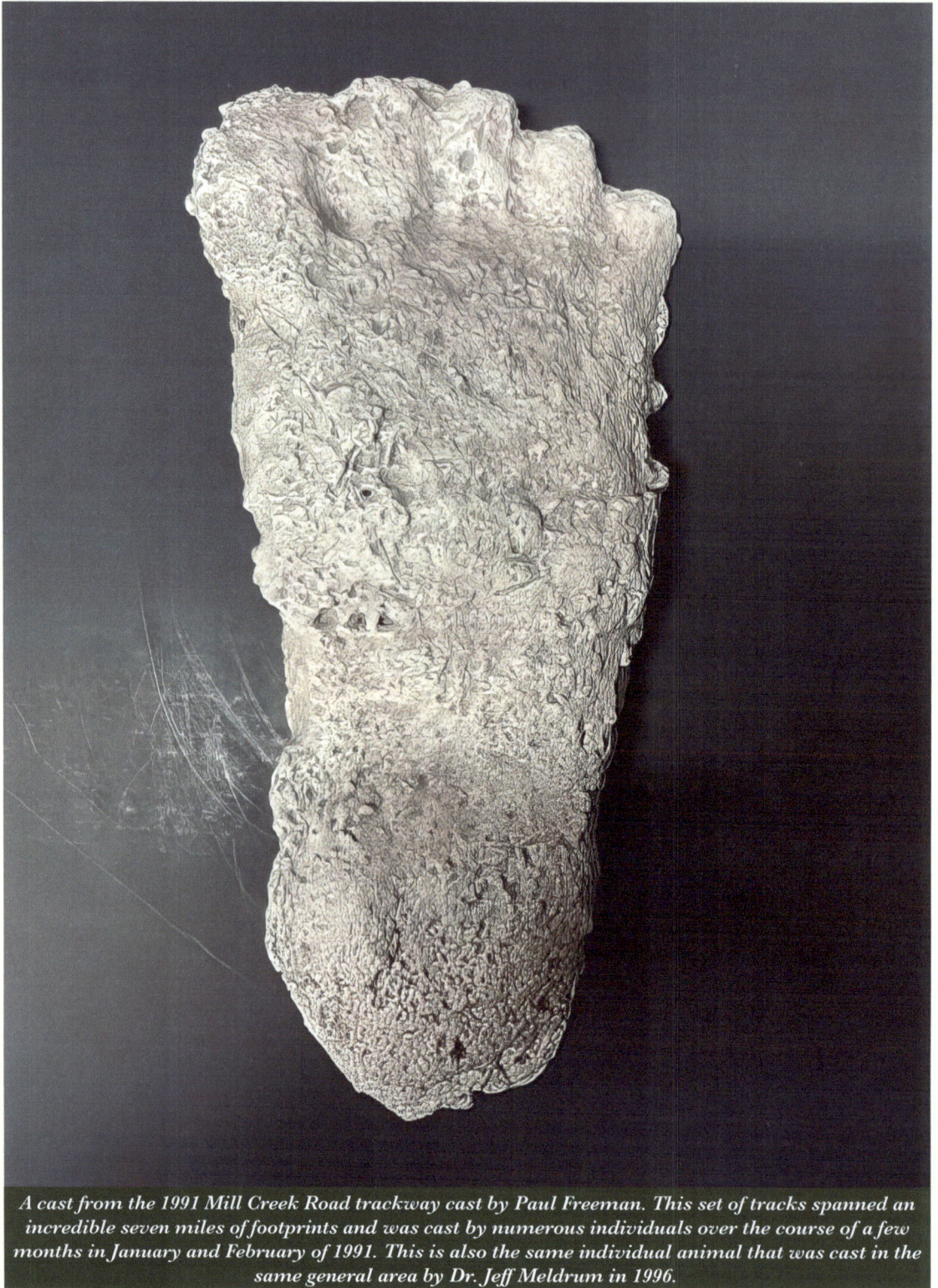

A cast from the 1991 Mill Creek Road trackway cast by Paul Freeman. This set of tracks spanned an incredible seven miles of footprints and was cast by numerous individuals over the course of a few months in January and February of 1991. This is also the same individual animal that was cast in the same general area by Dr. Jeff Meldrum in 1996.

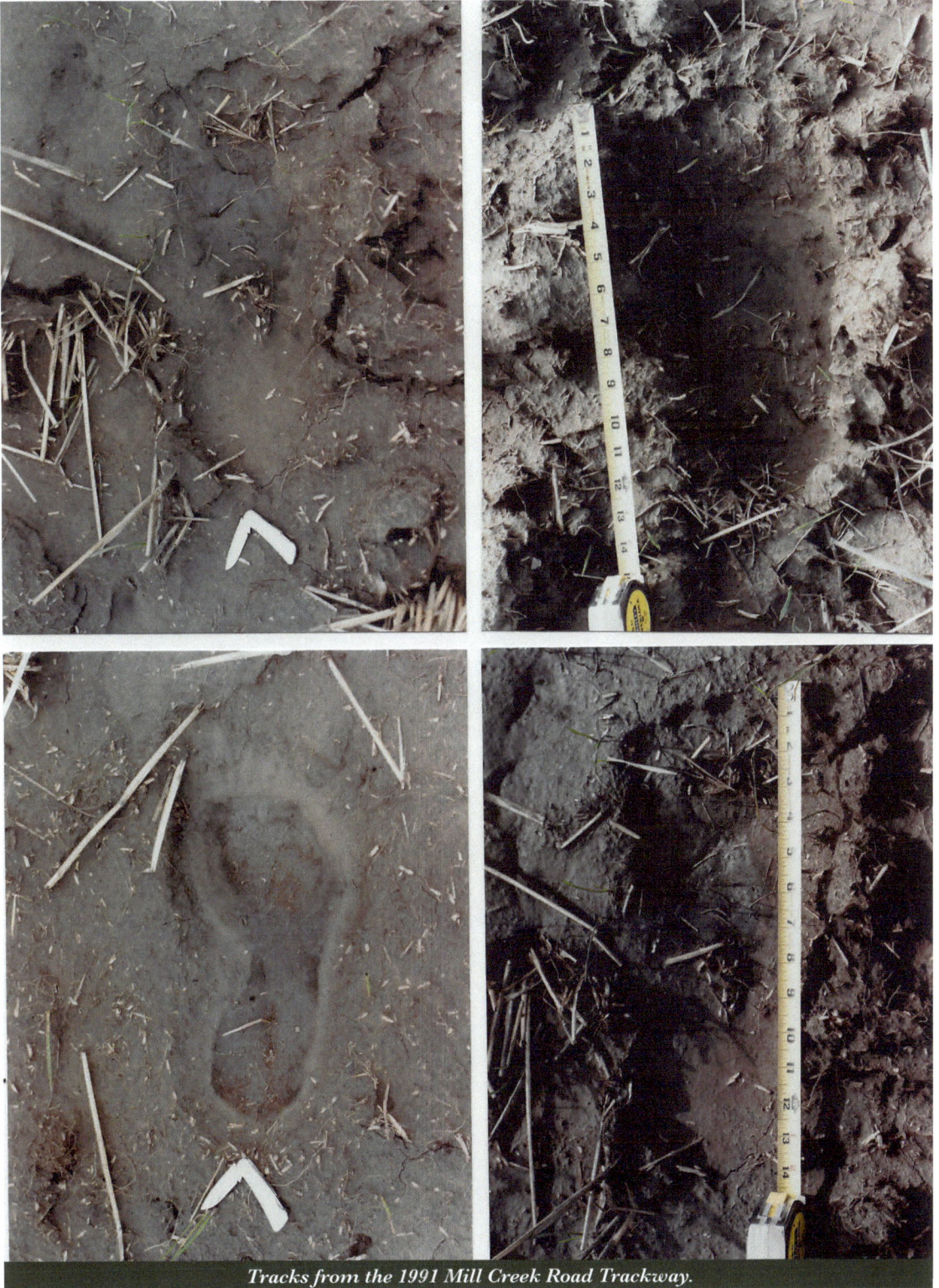

Tracks from the 1991 Mill Creek Road Trackway.

Another print taken from the Mill Creek Road trackway. This one was cast on January 23rd, 1991 by David Been.

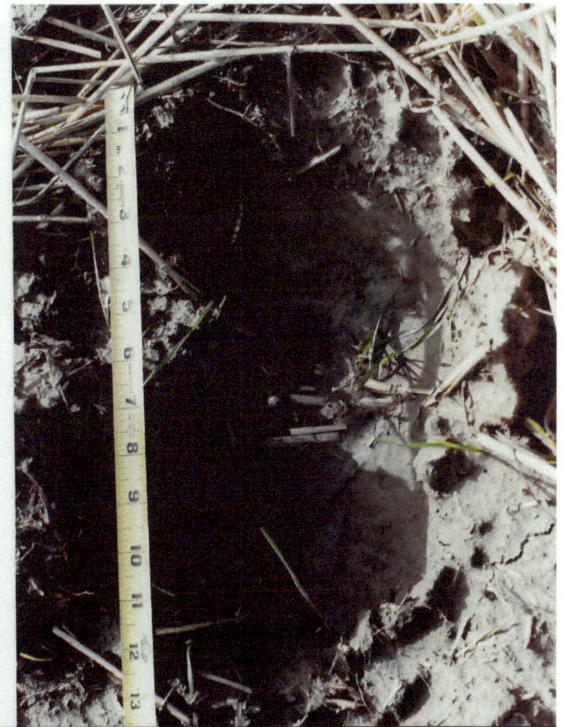

1991 Mill Creek Road. The "seven mile" tracks.

1991 Mill Creek Road.

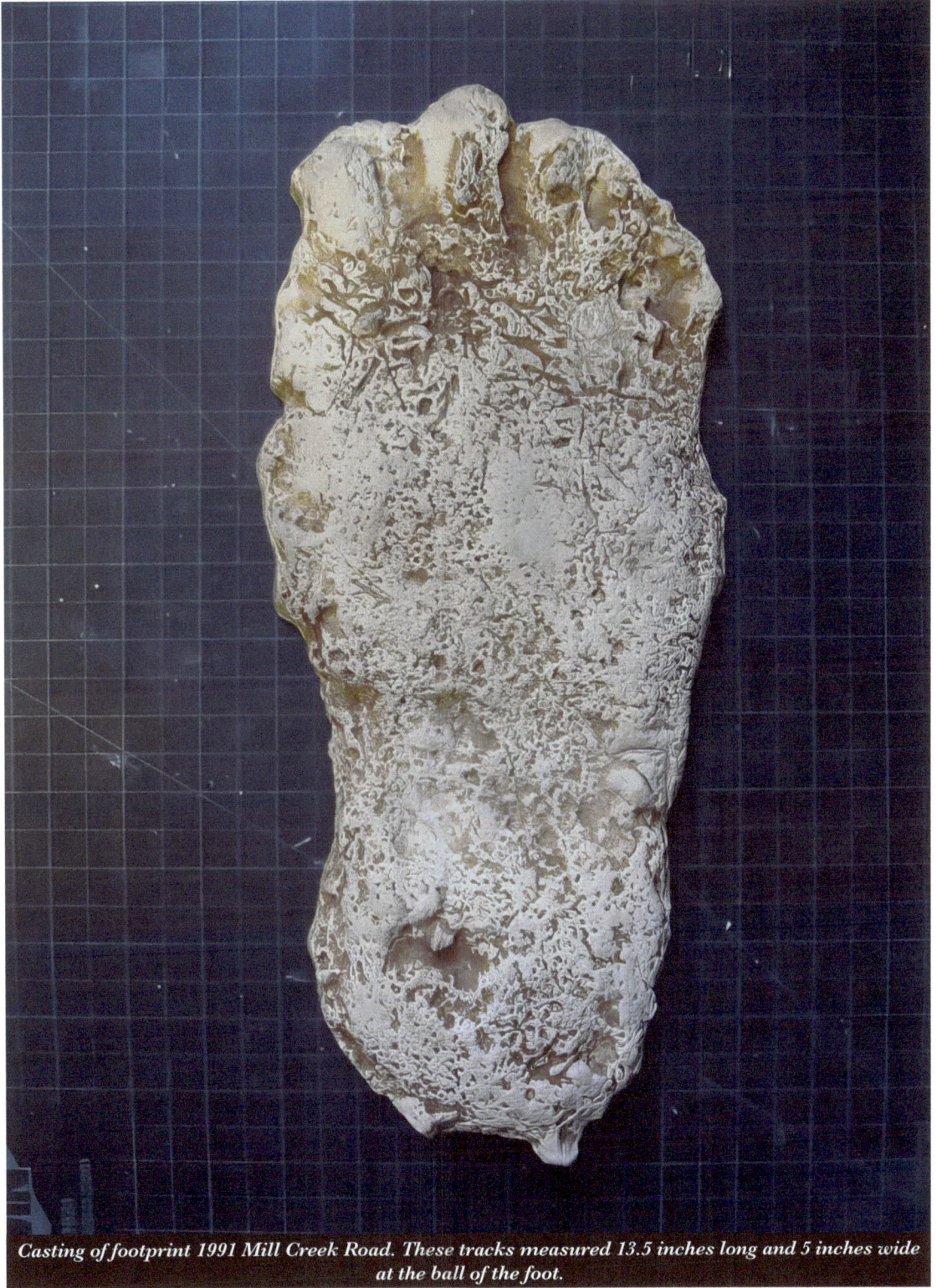

Casting of footprint 1991 Mill Creek Road. These tracks measured 13.5 inches long and 5 inches wide at the ball of the foot.

Paul Freeman, Wes Sumerlin, David Been, Vance Orchard, Bill Laughery, Greg May, Billy Fields and Dar Glasgow Addington were among those who investigated and made castings at the Mill Creek Road trackway in 1991.

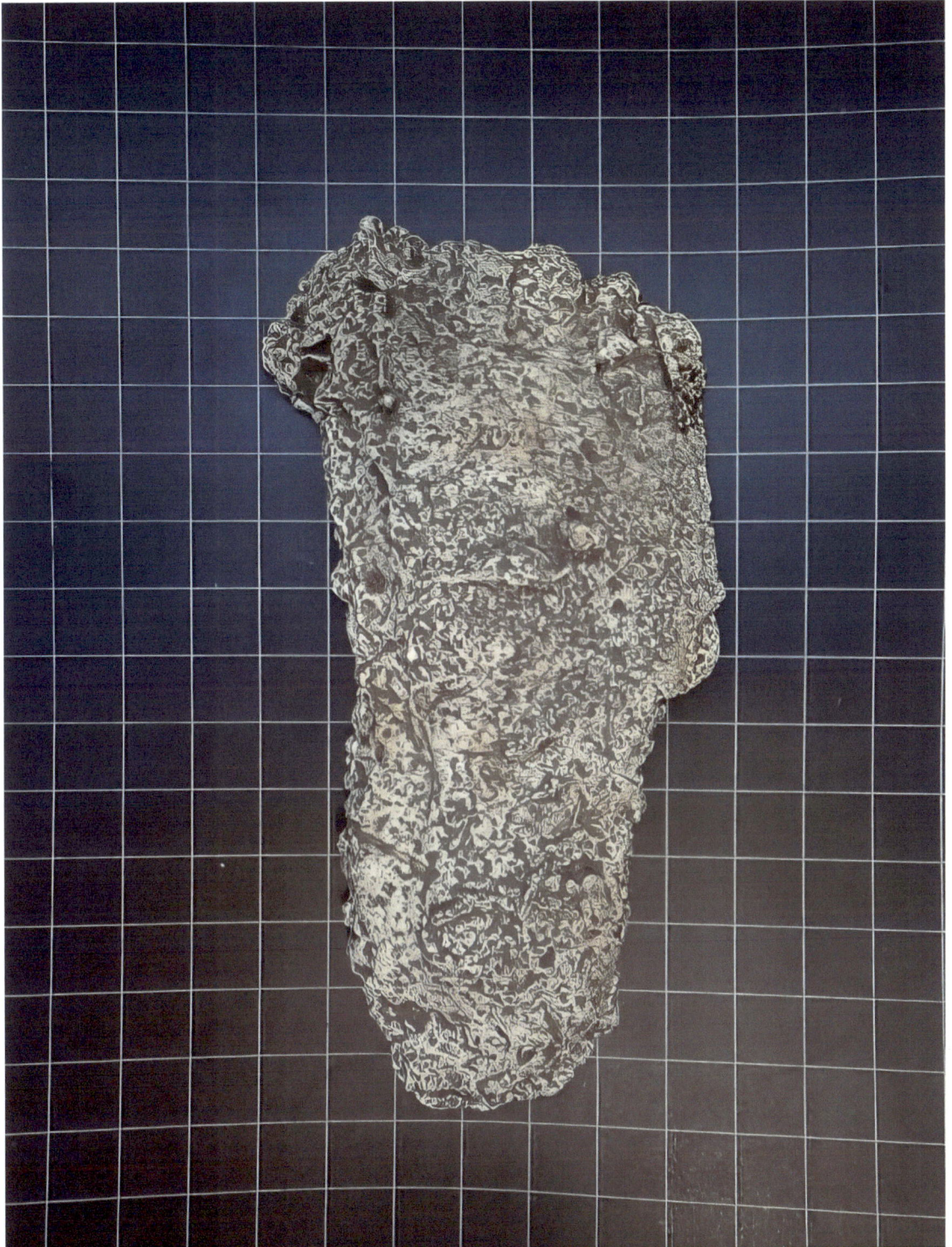

This cast was made by Dar Glasgow Addington in February of 1991 at the Mill Creek Road track find.

Abstract

SITE
-8 miles east of Walla Walla, Wa
-Date of inspection-1-25-91

DESCRIPTION
-5 continual sites inspected, no track interruption for 6-8 miles.
-Tracks first spotted 1-13-91.

PHYSICAL MATERIAL FOUND(1-25-91)
-6-8 miles of continual tracks. Hair, feces, vegetation disturbance.
-Tracks are 2 weeks old and located in varying terrain and sediment.

DISCLAIMER
Evaluation of impressions is based on known bipedal characteristics
and tendencies. This does not allow for unknown characteristics of
purported creature, "Bigfoot", or unknown prosthetic fabricative
features.

IMPRESSION EVALUATION CONCLUSIONS
For ease of reading, track source is referred to as "animal."
1.tracks were not hand tooled or stamped in any way.
2.tracks were made by a bipedal animal in normal expected movement
  mode.
3.animal is dominant left.
4.animal is male.
5.animal is 45-65 years of age.
6.animal has abnormal flexion in left ankle joint due to age/injury.
7.animal weighs between 300 and 600 pounds.
8.animal walked slowly with head and torso erect and chin forward.
9.tracks in cultivated field were made in the evening while the tracks
  near the orchard were made in daylight hours.

TRACKERS CONCLUSION
Tracks are valid-90%
Tracks are fake -10%

NARRATIVE
I am 90% certain that this site is valid and not fabricated. I allow
a 10% error for the possibility of the development of a fabricated
prosthetic with the necessary flexile characteristics inherent. In
addition to minor events, I base my 90% conclusion upon 4 major
points.
1.The animal moved with great care with regard to sight lines prior to
  the fruit ingestion at the orchard. Due to the amount of feces and
  the subsequent abnormal track patterns I concluded the the animal

became "punch drunk". This is a common event with bears. The
tracks display a great deal more weathering prior and during the
time spent at the orchard versus after. These tracks are as it

Field report by Greg May on the 1991 Mill Creek Rd. tracks pg.1.

should be, given southerly exposure and recorded temperature at that time. After the time spent at the orchard, the animal moved with little regard for sight lines but with purpose. While on difficult terrain, the animal moved with effort with regard to balance. This terrain has no specific exposure and these tracks were made at night. These tracks exhibit expected tendencies for a 6-8 mile traverse in a 18-22 hour elapsed time period.

2.Hip stride, general straddle and left foot inflection was consistent throughout travel given terrain.

3.A compressed gravel track indicated substantial weight and corresponding flexion.

4.Proper indicator pressure releases were evident in many instances. This rules out the possibility of hand tooling, barefoot human, or a flexible, crude prosthetic.

The following four individuals do not have the physical characteristics to fabricate these tracks by simply walking:
Paul Freeman
Duane Freeman
Swede Sumerlin
Wes Sumerlin

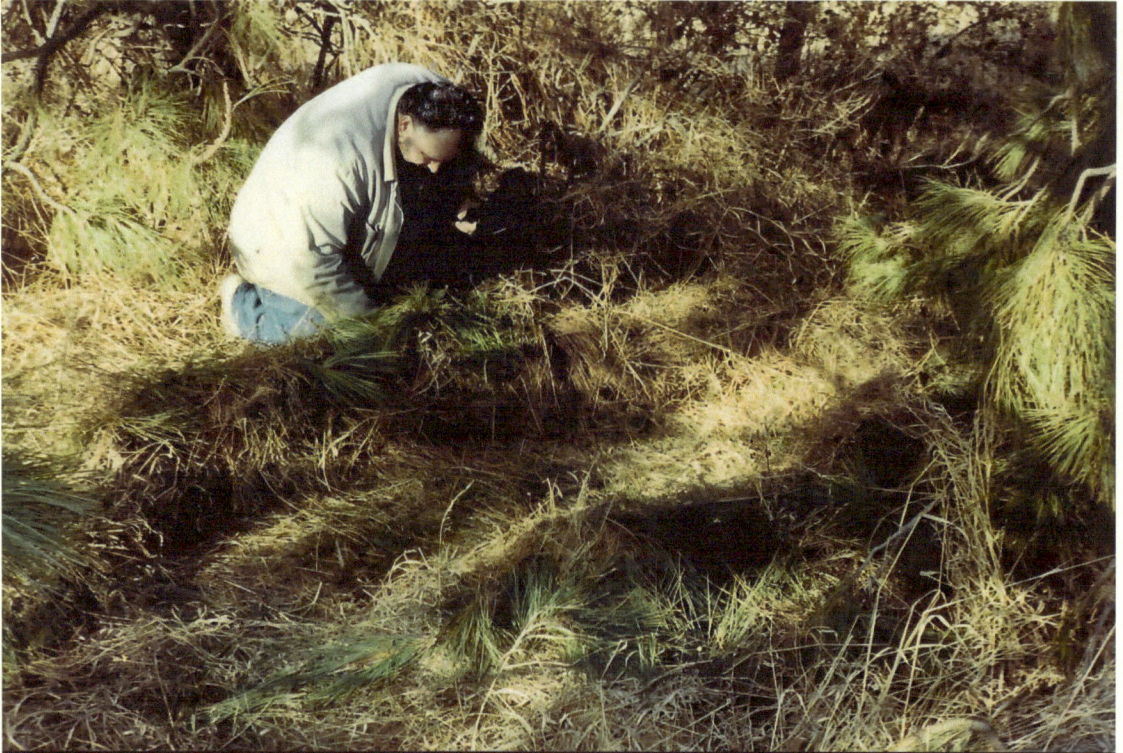

Paul investigating a possible nest, or bed 1991.

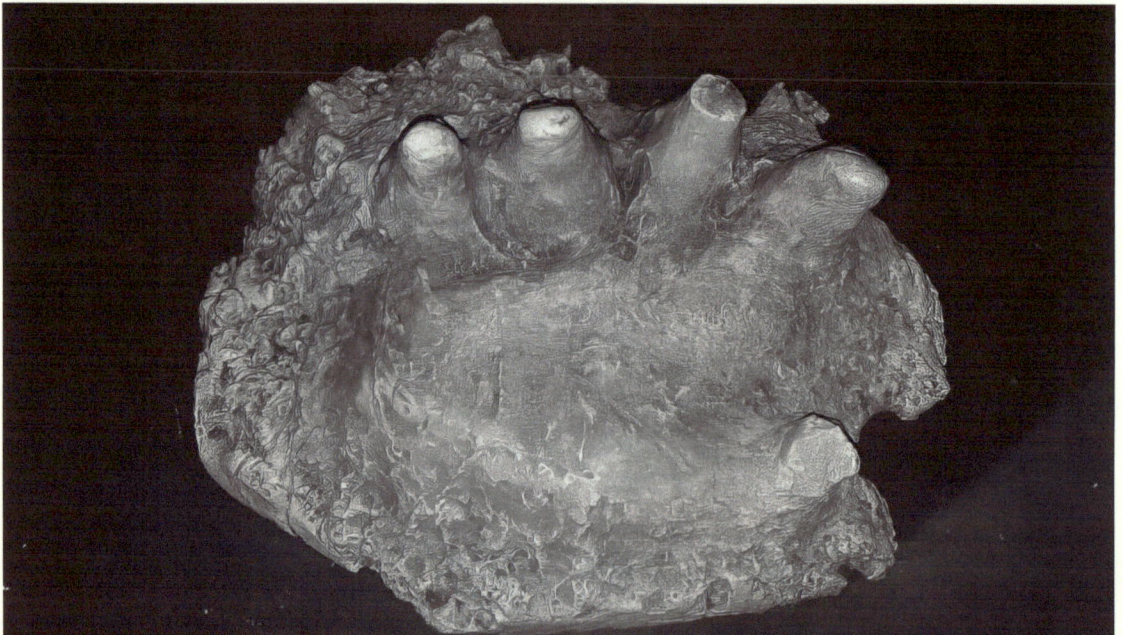

This hand was cast by Paul in 1994 at Biscuit Ridge and was taken from the side of a creek bank. The fingers had begun to fill with sediment and gives them the appearance of being very short.

I want to take a break from talking about my dad. Don't worry, we will get back to him in a moment. Right now I want to take some of your time to recognize my mother, Nancy Freeman. Born Nancy Cochran, she saw something in my father that was worth running away with him at the age of seventeen and getting married, having three children, and staying married to the man for thirty-six years at the time of his death. She was a strong woman who doesn't get the credit she deserves for the role she played in my dad's research. Almost every piece of evidence that my dad collected that was documented was done so by my mother. Almost every photo that was taken was documented on the back in my mother's handwriting. She put together photo albums, and display boards for his presentations, and typed all letters of correspondence for him. Not only did she do those things mentioned, but my mother also put up with him being gone all the time for fifteen years. She dealt with selling a home to support his research so he could work less and spend more time in the mountains. She dealt with the ridicule that came with being a Bigfoot researcher before it became a "cool" culture. Walla Walla, Washington was a small town in the 1980s and there were people that thought my dad was crazy. The forest service tried to discredit him. Good Morning America tried to discredit him.

You Damn Betcha

Nancy Cochran who would soon become Paul's wife, Nancy Freeman, in Camas, WA 1965 aged 17 years.

My father had a few good allies in those days, but without question, the biggest support he ever received came from my mother. A woman of tireless dedication, and tireless love, my mother was intelligent and kind. She was the backbone of our family. Nancy Freeman passed away at her home on August 6, 2011, after a long battle with cancer. Her children and grandchildren were with her, and I got to hold her hand. I hope there was love and peace in her final breath. She was a lovely and wonderful person and a supportive mother. My mom was the best.

There is another person who deserves credit for their role in all of this, and that is my older brother Duane. The oldest of the Freeman children, my brother was directly exposed to my dad's work in the field and his search for Bigfoot from the beginning. At eleven years older than me, Duane was sixteen years old and already an accomplished hunter by the time my dad had his first sighting that day in 1982. He spent a good deal of time over the next ten years helping my dad collect evidence, and he himself also took a great deal of ridicule. My brother was there helping my dad give a tour of the mountains to the crew of Good Morning America in 1987. And he was there when a crew member, proclaiming to be a seasoned expert, asked if he could fire my dad's rifle.

Duane

As one of the great Paul Freeman stories goes, that man ignored the warning from my dad when he said, as my brother can attest to, "get your goddam eye away from that scope" and ended up with eighteen stitches in his face where the rifle kicked back and busted his eye open. But my brother's biggest contribution, and the one he deserves credit for, came a year later on October 5th, 1988. While hunting with my dad near the Mill Creek Watershed my brother spotted and took photographs of a sasquatch coming out of the trees, and crossing a small clearing before heading back into cover up a nearby hillside. That was my brother's first and only sighting of a Bigfoot. As he snapped photographs with his camera, my father attempted to record video but could not get his camcorder to function properly. It was my brother that was there that day with my dad, and he experienced something with him that I never got the chance to have.

10/05/88

A black and white rendering of the zoomed-in photo.

This photo was taken on October 5th, 1988 by Duane Freeman while hunting with his dad, Paul Freeman.

At first glance the animal appears to have very skinny legs, but notice the light hitting the face and chest of the animal. It was walking into the sun and that glare off of its hair and the brush looks to be obscuring the leg as well and could attribute to this.

Friday, October 7, 1988

Photo courtesy of Paul Freeman

Duane Freeman took this picture Wednesday on the northwest side of the Mill Creek Watershed. His father, Paul Freeman, was with him at the time. The photo at right is an enlargement of the same photo, which Paul Freeman believes shows a 7½-foot-tall Bigfoot.

Freeman snaps Bigfoot photos

By KATHLEEN OBENLAND
Of the Union-Bulletin

Bigfoot hunter Paul Freeman has obtained what he considers his most significant Bigfoot evidence yet — photographs.

The pictures, showing a large, dark, humanlike shape moving away from the camera, were taken Wednesday between 10 and 10:30 a.m. on the northwest side of the Mill Creek Watershed by Freeman's son, Duane.

Several other pictures show the creature moving up a distant hillside.

"These are great," Freeman said this morning. "I know that people have said all long, 'He's lying. There's nothing there.' I know what I saw. I know what my son took pictures of."

He describes the creature as 7½ feet tall, 500 to 700 pounds, with a bulky build and extremely long arms. Its hair was dark, and the facial hair grayish.

Duane Freeman spotted it first in the distance.

"When this thing came out of the trees, he said he about fell over," Paul Freeman said. "He had thought the crashing through the trees was a deer."

The Bigfoot appeared to be moving toward the Freemans. Duane Freeman took a number of pictures, and Paul slapped some film into an old-fashioned movie camera and began filming — or so he thought. The movie pictures did not come out.

"(Bigfoot) came out of the trees about 150 yards from us," Freeman said. "It must have smelled us or something, because the way it was headed it should have come closer than that."

Freeman also made several plaster casts of the footprints the animal left.

Freeman goes into the watershed four to five times a week, looking for signs of the Bigfoot in the areas he believes they cross.

He has been hunting them since allegedly spotting one June 10, 1982, when he was employed as a watershed patrol rider for the Forest Service.

The newspaper article covering the photos taken by Duane on October 5th, 1988. Written for the Walla Walla Union Bulletin for Friday, October 7th, 1988.

Another photo taken by Duane shows the animal emerging from behind some brush. The trail or trackway can be clearly seen in this photo.

After crossing a small clearing the animal made its way up a nearby hillside and was photographed again crossing between two sets of trees.

A three-year-old Michael Freeman poses with a Bobcat, one of his father's recent kills, at their home in Camas, Washington in January of 1980.

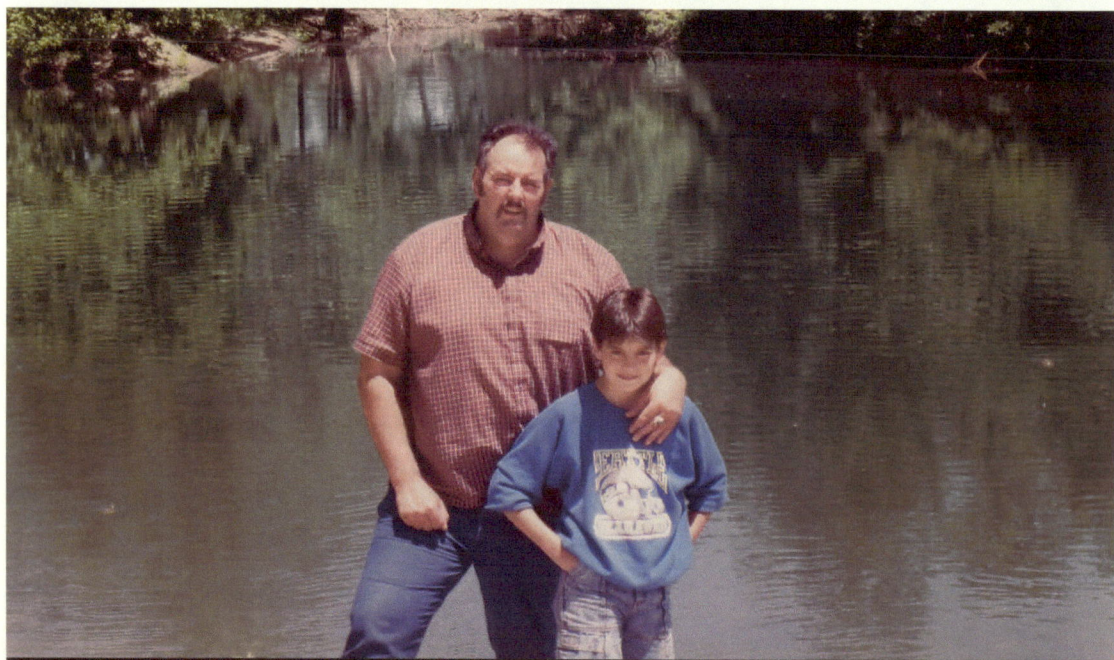

Paul Freeman poses with his son Michael during a trip to Missouri in 1988.

Michael Freeman at his home in Spokane, Washington. Michael took this photo in 2016 as an homage to a picture taken of his father in Camas, Washington in 1984.

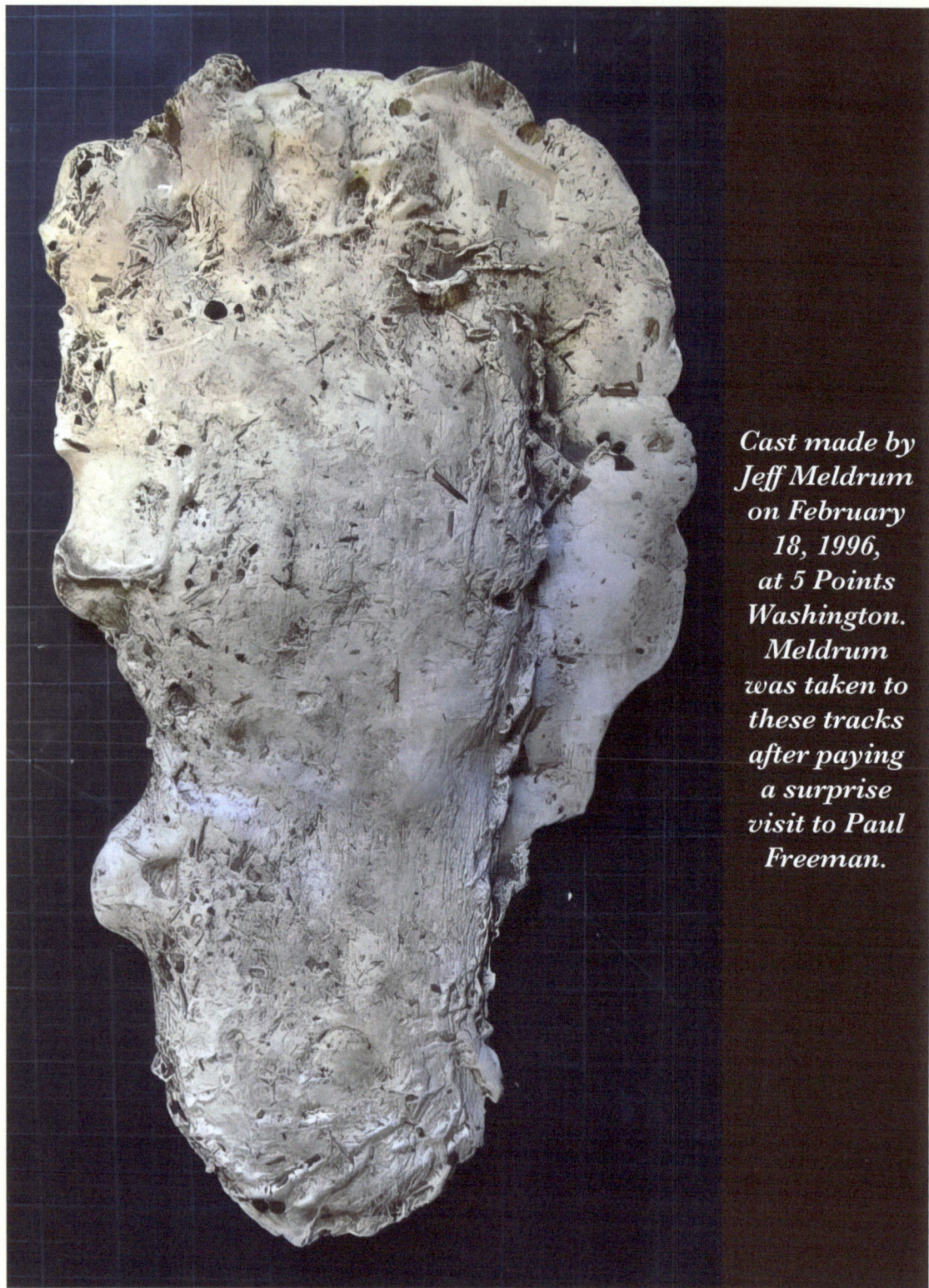

Cast made by Jeff Meldrum on February 18, 1996, at 5 Points Washington. Meldrum was taken to these tracks after paying a surprise visit to Paul Freeman.

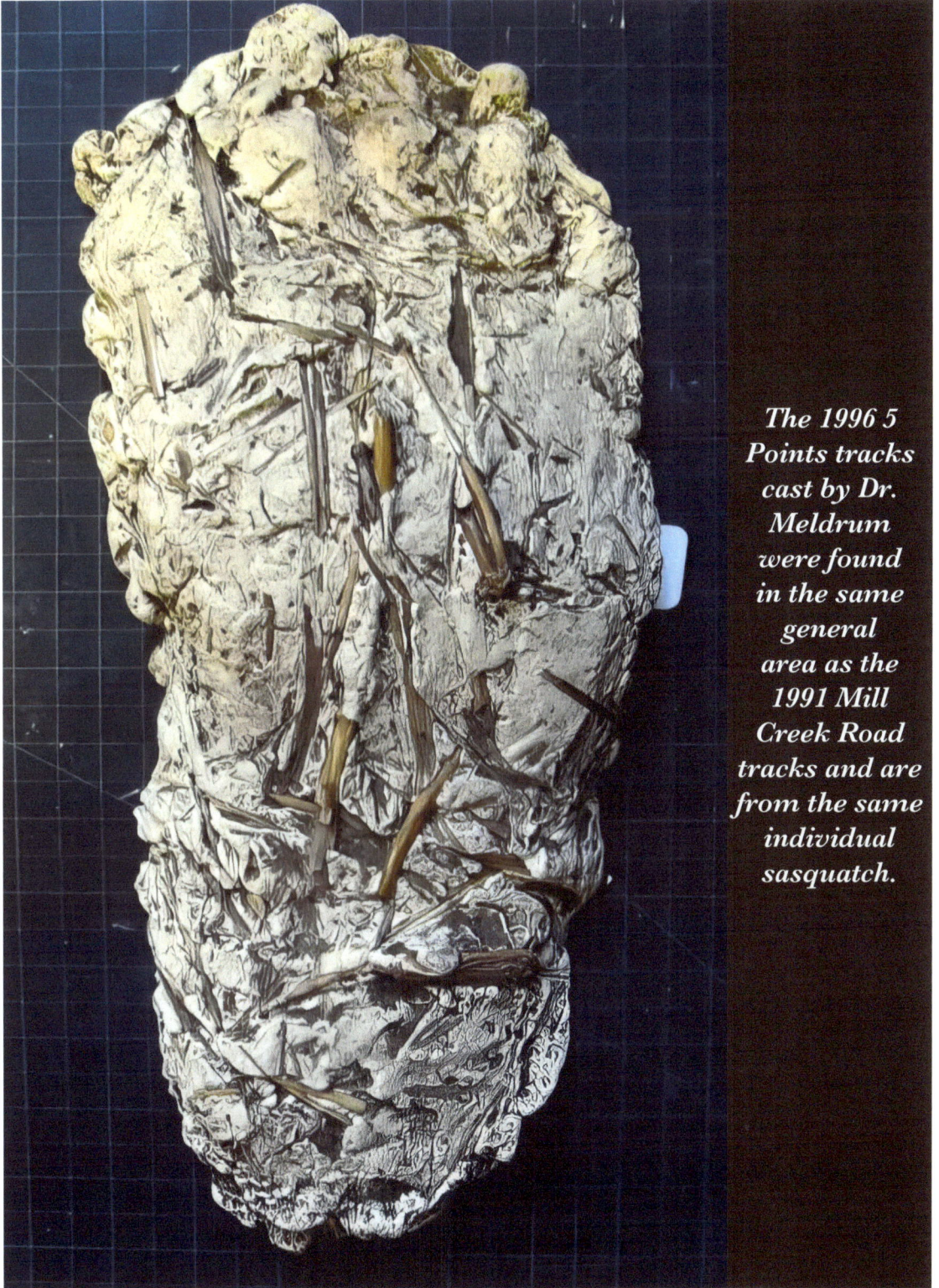

The 1996 5 Points tracks cast by Dr. Meldrum were found in the same general area as the 1991 Mill Creek Road tracks and are from the same individual sasquatch.

Paul Freeman in 1992 aged 49 years.

Cast made from a track found on August 4th, 1995. Location: Dry Creek, about 25 miles east of Walla Walla, Washington. Photo courtesy of Cliff Barackman.

Michael Freeman at his home in Spokane Washington, 2022.

BIGFOOT: THE NEW EVIDENCE

What is happening when a creature that is not supposed to exist makes tracks that could not possibly be faked?

By Jerome Clark

AT 11:30 on the morning of June 10, 1982, U.S. Forest Service patrolman Paul Freeman was driving through the Blue Mountains in the Walla Walla Ranger District of the Umatilla National Forest, which stretches across southeastern Washington and northeastern Oregon. When he spotted some elk he stopped his truck and got out to pursue the animals on foot; he wanted to see if there were any calves among them.

As he walked down the old logging trail called Tiger Canyon Road he certainly didn't realize he was approaching the most shattering event of his life, that he was about to spark new interest in one of this country's most enduring scientific mysteries and provide investigators with powerful new evidence for the reality of a creature that is not supposed to exist.

As Freeman rounded a bend he noticed a "stench" and at the other side of the turn saw something coming down a bank through thick vegetation.

When the figure stepped into the clearing, Freeman froze and stared in disbelief at an "enormous creature" which stared back at him. For a few seconds the two studied each other from a distance of 150 to 200 feet, then fled in opposite directions.

Until that fateful meeting Freeman, a veteran outdoorsman who had started working for the Forest Service only the month before, openly ridiculed Bigfoot reports. But the thing he had seen had

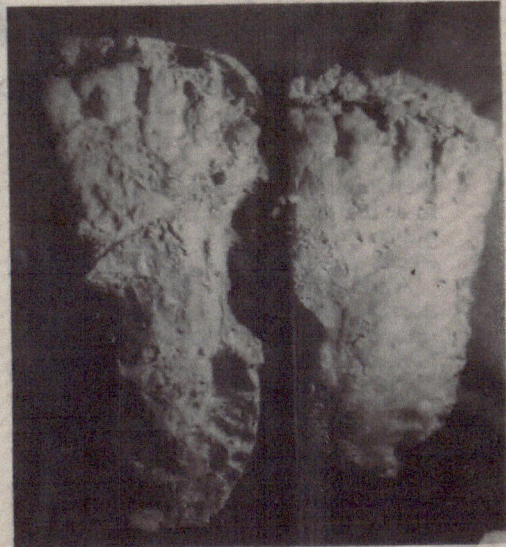

Cast on right was taken at site of Paul Freeman's Bigfoot encounter. One on left is the same creature but from watershed site a few miles away.

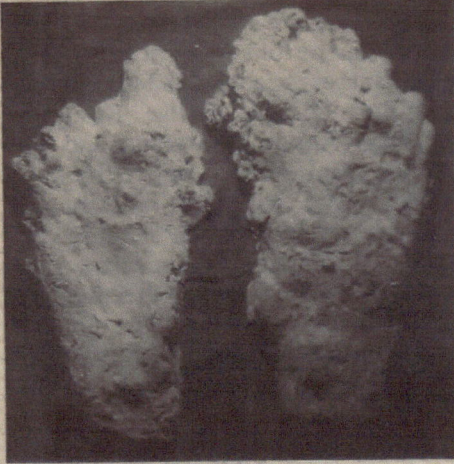

One of two creatures that figure in the Umatilla National Forest events left prints in watershed but unlike its companion was never observed.

an apelike appearance, stood about 8½ feet tall and was covered with reddish-brown hair. Its long arms stretched all the way to its knees. It had a "peaked crown" (sagittal crest) on its head. It matched in every particular the classic physical characteristics of the fabled hairy giant of the Pacific Northwest.

"I could see the muscles of his legs when he walked," Freeman told investigators soon afterwards. "I could see the muscles in the arms and shoulders. It just plain scared me and I've never been scared in the woods before. This thing was real. It was big enough to tear the head right off your shoulders if it wanted to."

The encounter was especially frightening because the hair on the creature's neck and head stood up three times "like a dog's back," causing Freeman to fear "it was going to come at me."

He was positive it was not a bear. "I see bears all the time in the watershed," he said. "I just stand still and they walk off . . . . I never saw anything like this in that area . . . . I've been working in the wild all of my life and I know a bear or a man in a gorilla suit when I see one—and that's not what I saw. I still can't sleep at night thinking about it."

The badly shaken patrolman immediately notified his superiors in Walla Walla, Wash., and two hours later a group of Forest Service personnel arrived at the site, located in Oregon near the Washington border. They found 21 footprints measuring 14 inches long by seven inches wide; they took three casts and some pictures of the prints.

One member of the party, Fire Management Officer Wayne Long, has lived in Washington and Oregon forests for over three decades, but this was, he said, "the first time I've ever seen a foot like this. I don't think this thing is man-

This close-up of print of Individual I (Bigfoot that left tracks but was not seen) shows left foot. Prints show bottom, not top, of feet.

55

made. If it had been a single track or two tracks, I might dispute it. But 21 tracks?''

Even more impressive, however, was the fact that the prints were over an inch deep in the hard ground of the unpaved logging road.

On June 14 the Walla Walla station released a statement recounting the details of Freeman's sighting and remarking that ''no determination can be made'' concerning the creature's identity. The Forest Service said it had no further plans to investigate. Nonetheless, four days later it reported that on the 16th, Freeman and Patrolman Bill Epoch had discovered about 40 new tracks in the Mill Creek Watershed on the Washington side of the border. On the 17th, Joel Hardin, a U.S. Border Patrol tracking expert, examined the prints and declared they were hoaxes. He pointed out that they showed evidence of dermal ridges, which animals don't have. Hardin did not mention that higher primates— monkeys, apes and human beings—do have such ridges on their toes and fingers.

Freeman, who accompanied Hardin to the site, disputed Hardin's conclusions. ''I'm just as much a professional tracker as he is,'' Freeman said. ''He's good at tracking people but I've been tracking animals for 30 years.''

One problem with Hardin's hoax hypothesis is that the area in which the prints were found is a restricted site inaccessible to the public and cut off from any roads. A hoax would have been simpler to perpetrate in a place more easily accessible such as the Tiger Creek location where Freeman supposedly had his sighting.

But Freeman's colleagues are convinced that he told the truth and that the footprints associated with his report are genuine. District Office Resources Manager Randy Dohrmann and Fire Management Officer Long testify to his integrity and they recall how shocked and frightened Freeman had appeared to be. If the event was a hoax, Long insisted, it was a hoax *on* Freeman, not by him—but even so, how could a hoaxer in a Sasquatch suit leave inch-deep prints in hard ground?

The day after Freeman's sighting, the Umatilla County (Oregon) Sheriff's Department sent a five-person team of volunteers to the Tiger Creek area. The searchers were not looking for a Bigfoot but for the body of a boy who had disappeared the previous fall. They were brought to the site because the sheriff's officers noted Freeman's report of a ''stench,'' which they thought might be from a decaying corpse. The sheriff did not even inform the searchers that the odor had been noted in association with a Bigfoot sighting. Although the team found neither stench nor body, it did make another discovery.

According to Art Snow, a Milton-Freewater, Oreg., businessman who headed the team, the search party was able to follow the tracks beyond the 21 found by the Forest Service people. In fact, Snow claimed, tracks were discernible for three-quarters of a mile. The team made a cast of one of the better prints.

''It would not be possible to fake the tracks without a helicopter,'' Snow says. ''We assumed Freeman was telling the truth and we could find no evidence whatsoever to contradict that assumption. I'm not saying that there is or is

Dermal ridges, including sweat glands (little holes between some ridges), are clearly visible on all casts taken at the two Walla Walla sites.

not a Bigfoot but all evidence verifies his story."

In July, Paul Freeman, still distraught from his experience and upset at all the publicity it had received, resigned from the Forest Service.

*   *   *

AT THE TIME the Walla Walla Bigfoot incidents were occurring, anthropologist Grover Krantz was out of the country. One of the places he visited was China, where he met with scientists who are investigating reports there of "wildmen," apelike creatures somewhat akin to our own Bigfoot.

An associate professor of anthropology at Washington State University, Dr. Krantz, who has spent 15 years studying reports, tracks and other Bigfoot

evidence, is America's leading scientific authority on the phenomenon. It is perhaps ironic that he was among the last to hear of what may well be the most important Bigfoot-related incident yet to occur.

Krantz learned of it shortly after his return to the United States when he visited the home of J. Richard Greenwell, secretary of the International Society of Cryptozoology,* of which Krantz is a founding member. After Greenwell described the incident to him, Krantz promised to investigate it as soon as he got back to Washington.

* The ISC, formed in January 1982 at a meeting held at the Smithsonian Institution, is an organization of scientists interested in reports of "hidden animals." Its address is Box 43070, Tucson, Ariz. 85733.

Forensics expert who has studied dermal ridges on casts believes such effects are impossible to fake. Top authorities are continuing investigation.

Soon afterwards Wayne Long furnished Krantz with four casts from both the Tiger Creek and Mill Creek Watershed areas. Krantz also secured the print Art Snow had cast the day after Freeman's reported encounter.

Some weeks later, in a summary of conclusions from his investigation, Krantz wrote that the prints were from "two individuals." The first of these, represented by two casts, one of each foot, had a big toe larger than that in the average Bigfoot track. The second specimen had a "splayed-out second toe."

Aside from these distinguishing features, the prints were much alike and typical of those associated with Bigfoot reports. The feet were about 15 inches long and the toes were more nearly equal in size than a human being's would be. The arches were nearly flat and a "double ball" was visible at the base of the big toe.

Adding to the prints' credibility was the fact that there were no human prints around the Bigfoot tracks. The distance between them suggested that whoever made them had a *long* stride. Moreover, they were so deeply impressed into the ground that most investigators believed it would have taken over 600 pounds of force to make them; yet there was no evidence to suggest the presence of the kinds of mechanical devices necessary to fake this effect. The more likely explanation is that these were indeed the footprints of two huge, heavy figures.

But the most dramatic evidence of all came not from Krantz but from another specialist who studied the prints. Krantz had observed that because of the unprecedented clarity of the prints, dermal ridges, fine lines about half a

millimeter apart in the skin of the feet, were visible—the first time this had ever happened on Bigfoot prints. The same kinds of ridges when found on the hand are called fingerprints.

Krantz presented this evidence to Benny D. Kling, a forensics expert at the Law Enforcement Academy in Douglas, Wyo. Kling's examination revealed that the dermal-ridge patterns were those of higher primates but the foot and toe shapes were different from a human being's or an ape's. Some of the ridges were worn smooth in exactly the places one would expect from someone or something that had walked barefoot for a long time. The patterns of ridges and furrows were so intricate and so anatomically correct that in Kling's view a hoax was simply not possible.

At a press conference held at the University of British Columbia on October 22, 1982, Krantz reported the results of his and Kling's studies of the prints. "It is beyond the ability of anyone to fake these ridges," he declared. "These may be the best set of prints of a Sasquatch ever obtained."

On November 2, 1982, in a letter to a number of America's leading anthropologists, Krantz described briefly the results of his and Kling's work on the prints and solicited his colleagues' help in the continuing investigation. Subsequently Krantz sent copies of the letter to forensics specialists and fingerprint experts.

The response from the anthropologists has ranged from total rejection to cautious interest but none has volunteered his services. This is hardly surprising since anthropologists traditionally have been more interested in keeping their distance from Bigfoot

BIGFOOT: THE NEW EVIDENCE   59

than in considering the evidence for its existence. Many of the forensics specialists, on the other hand, have been impressed, even excited by the new evidence and some of the top people in the field are now actively involved in the research.

The prints, Krantz remarks wryly, "come from a higher primate that doesn't exist. So we have an interesting problem here."

Meanwhile Paul Freeman, whose sighting started it all, has become a man obsessed. Stung by the ridicule to which he was subjected after his sighting was publicized, he is determined to prove that he told the truth about his experiences—and the way to do that, he reasons, is to prove Bigfoot exists. So he spends most of his spare time with his son roaming the area where he had his encounter with the creature. He hopes to see it again. But this time he is armed and he intends to supply the world with the only proof he thinks it will accept: a Bigfoot body.

Krantz seems to have something of the same idea. He plans to return to the site this summer in order, he says, to "obtain a specimen." Asked if this means he intends to kill one, he replies vaguely that the International Society of Cryptozoology has no policy on "hunting or not hunting."

In any case, it looks very much as if the long controversy over Bigfoot has taken a major new turn. Body or no body, a breakthrough may be imminent and all of us, scientists and lay persons, may be forced to live with a disquieting fact: that we share the North American continent with strange hairy animals which are uncomfortably close relatives of ours.

Vance Orchard poses with casts from the Freeman collection. Paul and Vance were good friends, and upon Paul's death in 2003 Vance wrote his obituary.

Duane was my dad's right-hand man for many years, and if you listen to my father's tapes he speaks of him often. There did come a time though when his feelings would change, and my brother took a step back. He would tell my father that he was tired of the talk, and of the ridicule. He no longer wanted to talk to news people, and wouldn't be helping my dad as much anymore. This was around 1990, and when you listen to my father speak of it you can tell that there is a little hurt in his voice. But much like myself, who was starting to experience the same feelings at that time, my dad said he understood and never held it against either of us. My brother and I see one another when we can, and honestly, it's probably not enough. Most recently we came together to mourn the death of our sister Linda, who was tragically taken all too soon from this life in a motorcycle accident on June 5th, 2022. But even in those times of sadness, there was a chuckle to be had sharing stories of our old man, and reminiscing about our childhood.

He Won't Be Going with Me Anymore

"Likely The Best Sasquatch Tracker of All Time" - Thom Powell

Born August 10, 1943, in Sanger California, Paul Freeman was raised in Iowa, and then the hills of Missouri. My dad learned at a young age to shoot, and to hunt, to track and to trap. His father, my Grandfather Louis Freeman was a dairy farmer who also raised pigs. I've heard tell of large barrels full of corn mash out behind the barn that was supposedly used as feed for the hogs, or so my Grandmother was told, but neither my dad nor my older brother Duane could ever remember eating any pork. One thing my dad always remembered though is running hounds. My dad and his father ran coons and bear with hounds, and Louis Freeman was known as a strict and effective trainer of dogs that produced efficient hunters and loyal animals. Louis Freeman also produced my father, who was as efficient a hunter as one can be. Trained to hunt and track, he was also a proficient trapper and there were many winters gotten through on wild game at the dinner table and the sale of pelts.

For a period of time, my dad was a paid hunting guide, leading men with money, and showing them where to shoot so they could take trophies home. That line of work did not sit well with him, it was short-lived and quickly left. After my Grandfather passed my parents moved back west for good with my brother and sister in tow. I can remember the first and only time I ever visited my Grandmother in Missouri. My father took me to see her when I was eleven years old and upon arriving she handed my dad a single shot .22 and asked him to get something for the stew, for dinner. That night we ate squirrel and apple pie, the latter of which caused my hand to get belted when I touched it before it was time to be served. Oh well, she was a mean woman anyway.

I never knew much of the old timers personally. I met them all, well almost. I've been around Bob Titmus, Peter Byrne, John Green, and Rene Dahinden. I spent a lot of time with Grover Krantz and can vividly remember his office and lab at Washington State University in Pullman, Washington. I never met Roger Patterson, as he had died in 1972, five years before I was even born and ten years before my dad even became a believer. And I've yet to meet Bob Gimlin. But I would be hard-pressed to think of anyone who has ever done this that was more qualified from a hunter's perspective than my dad. As a true mountain man, there was no better. The only person that I would even consider to be close would be Wes Sumerlin. Wes was an old man when I knew him, but he was one hell of a tracker and a cowboy. Wes and my dad made a pretty good team for some time. Separate but together, they lent both expertise and credibility to one another and formed a group of researchers in the Blues that also included Vance Orchard, David Been, Bill Laughery and female pioneer Dar Glasgow Addington. They were not only experienced and determined, but they were also in the center of a literal hot spot for Bigfoot activity. I've heard of someone saying in regards to my dad, that he was either the luckiest bigfooter that ever lived, or he was a hoaxer. It is neither, and quite the opposite actually. Paul Freeman was skilled in what he was doing, and he knew the area as well as anyone ever has. He put in the time, four to five days a week, sometimes more, sometimes overnight, or even a week at a time for fifteen years. He was the perfect guy in the perfect place at the perfect time.

It's Just Not Gonna Happen

Scenic Loop Road runs just outside of Walla Walla, Washington. As its name would imply it is quite a pretty drive with some fantastic views of the wheat fields in the valley below and the impending mountains that hold so many great mysteries. Paul Freeman received a message in late January 1995 that would lead to quite a discovery off of the Scenic Loop as well. An account told by some college students that were up there having a good time prompted an investigation that would, much like the 91' Mill Creek Rd. tracks before, and the 96' 5 Points tracks to follow, turn up another outstanding trackway in a familiar area. Sets of tracks from both an adult and what is thought to be a juvenile would be tracked here through very wet and muddy conditions. The adult tracks measure in at 13.5 -14 inches, and the juvenile tracks around 11-12 inches.

Although these tracks were investigated and documented by numerous individuals there are no known casts from this trackway that I have been able to locate at the moment. This would also be the beginning of the end for both my father's research and his physical mobility.

Mormon Grade Scenic Loop 1995

I'd like to think that what Paul Freeman left behind, his legacy, would stand the test of time. I'd like to think that the evidence he collected, from the Dermals in 1982, all the way past the Deduct Spring footage he captured in 92' would stand as cornerstones of proof for the existence of Bigfoot. That he himself would stand as proof for the existence of Bigfoot. Unfortunately, the world of scientific proof doesn't work that way, and we all know what it is going to take to finally settle this debate. When that day comes, if it ever comes, I will not celebrate. I do not want to see one killed, or captured. I quite enjoy the mystery actually. My father, who was vocal about "putting one on a table" after his first encounter, changed his mind later in life, realizing they were something special. And by the time of his death in 2003, Paul Freeman was a strong advocate for their protection and for them to just be left alone.

In The Crosshairs

So I sit here and I write this, and I think to myself what would my dad want? If Paul Freeman were still alive to see the popularity of today's Bigfoot entertainment culture, what would he want? And it is a clear conclusion. I know that he wouldn't want anything. He didn't have anything to prove to anyone. He shared his knowledge with the world, and very few believed him. And now he's gone. But I'm still here. And his evidence is still here. There are people like Cliff Barackman, and Jeff Meldrum, and Doug Hajicek along with myself and others who are continuing to study that evidence and present it to a whole new generation of people in hope of expanding that knowledge and understanding.

A Million Miles

So, if Paul Freeman were still alive today he may not ask for it, but he would certainly deserve to see it happening. My dad would deserve this book, and I'm giving it to him. It is one last thing that I can give to my dad. And it is in turn something that he can give to the Grandchildren that never got to meet him. My sister-in-law Arianna said something to me that made me stop and think, as I had never thought about it from that point of view before. She said that maybe my dad's story and this book, if nothing else, will help to validate someone's feelings who has had an experience and is afraid to talk about it. That it might let them know that it's alright, and they are not crazy, or weird, or alone. So I will try and preserve Paul Freeman's legacy, and along the way maybe he can inspire someone as well. This book is for my father, my very own Superman.

A Couple Ladies

So what was it like growing up with Paul Freeman as my dad? That's an easy answer, I didn't know any better. He was just my dad and just the same as anyone elses. We didn't always have money, there were some rough times, and it is well documented by his own admission that he was gone more than he should have been. We may have missed him from time to time, or even worried about him, but we never suffered for lack of love. And that is probably the single best thing that I could ever say about my father. Despite everything else, who he was, how he was seen, or what he was famous for, he was always my dad first, and I never once felt unloved. That is the ultimate testament to Paul Freeman. We all grow up with the hand we are dealt. You grew up with the parents you had and the challenges that presented. I grew up with mine. It just so happens that I also grew up with Bigfoot.

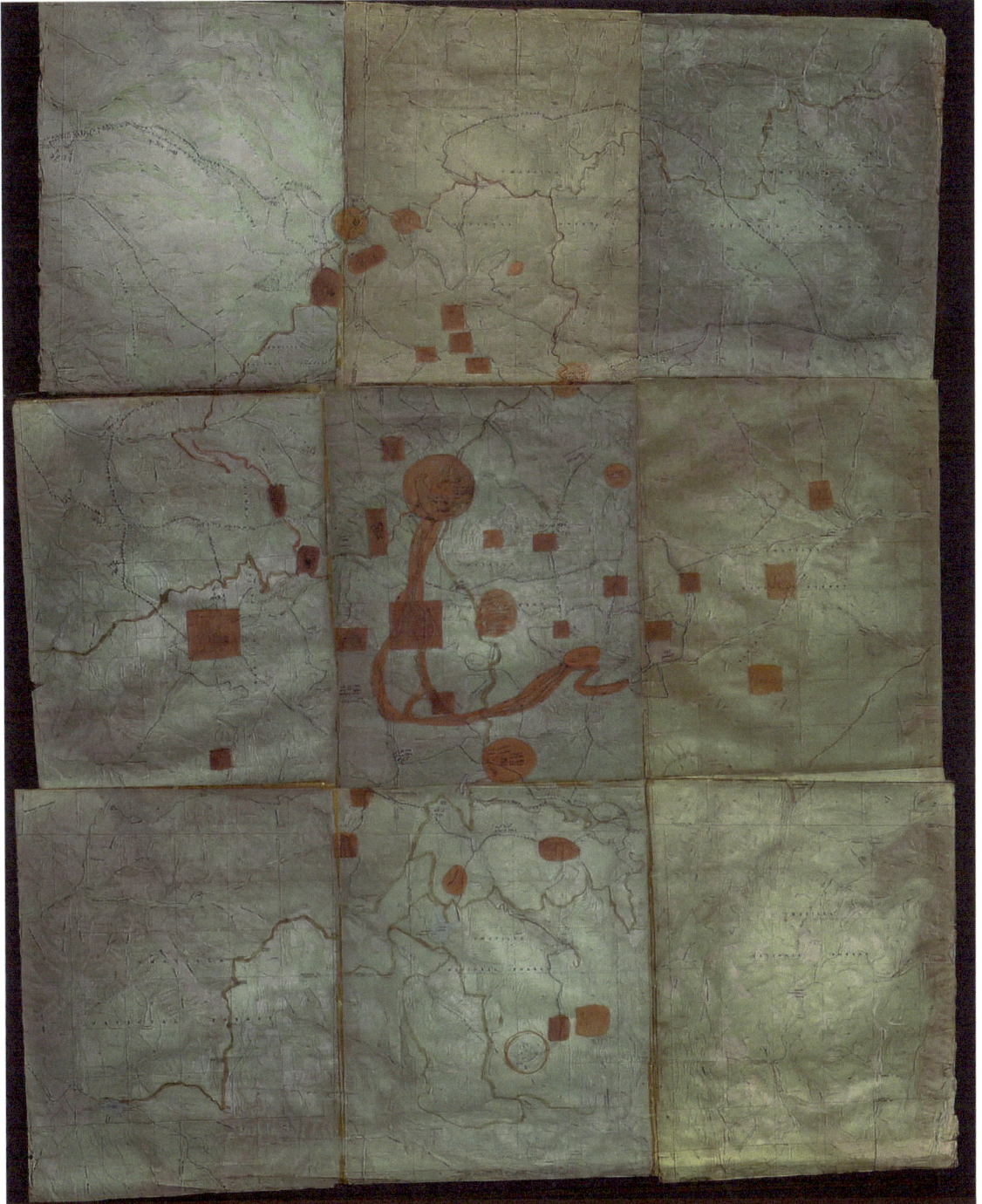

The Paul Freeman Map. This Forest Service map was kept by Paul for over 10 years and has writing from himself as well as other individuals. It was used to track footprint finds and sighting locations, along with other evidence, in hopes of deciphering movement patterns in the area. This map currently resides under the care of Cliff Barackman.

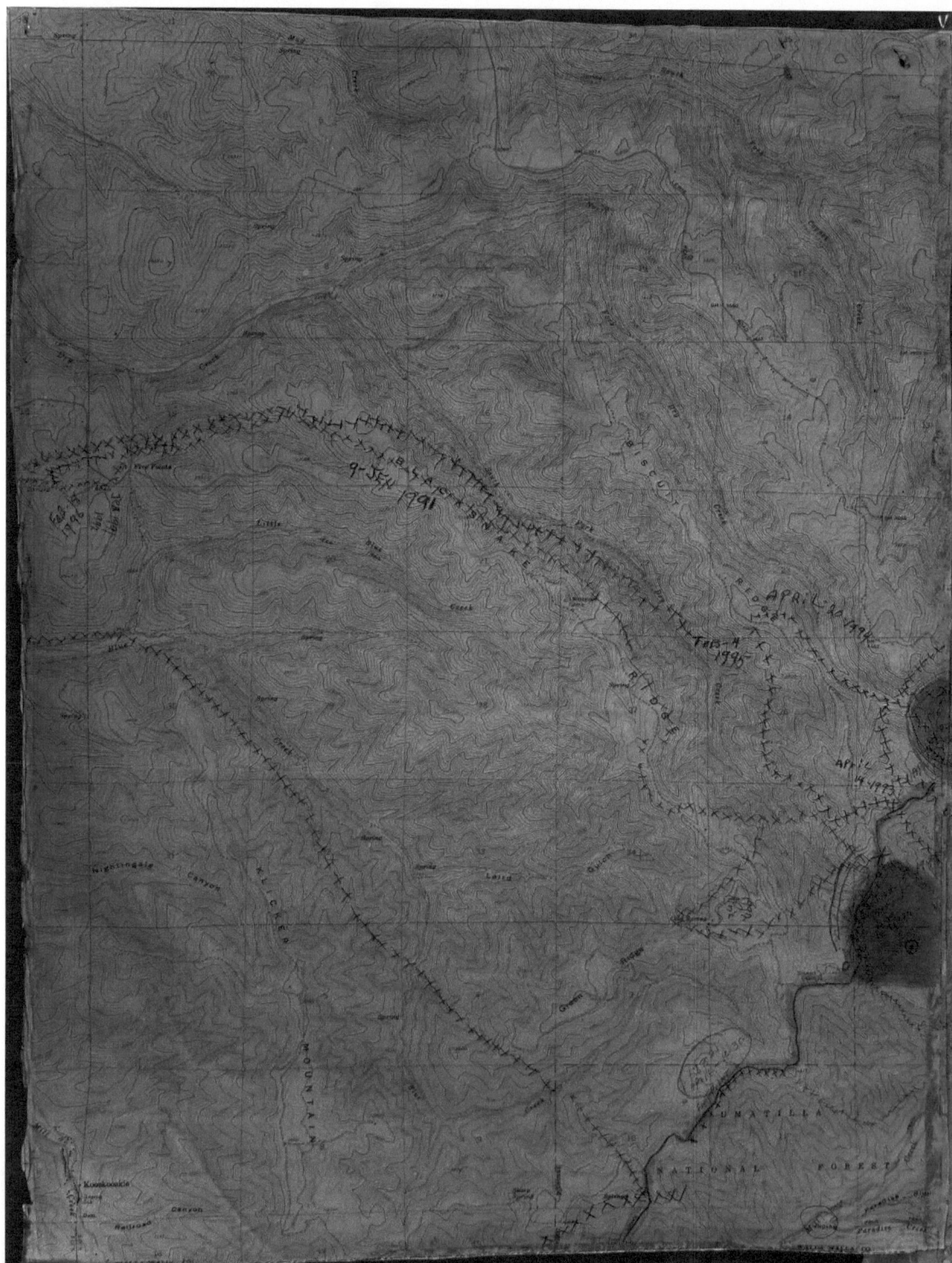

*Freeman Map individual section view 1 - The X's on the map represent tracks
found and the presumed routes the Bigfoot were using.*

Freeman Map individual section view 2 - Circles on the map that contain solid dots in the center show locations of sightings. Ovals without center dots show the location of possible beds or nests found.

Freeman Map individual section view 3 - This section of the map shows the Wenaha-Tucannon wilderness area.

Freeman Map individual section view 4 - The large dark circle to the right of this section is the location of Freeman's initial sighting on June 10, 1982.

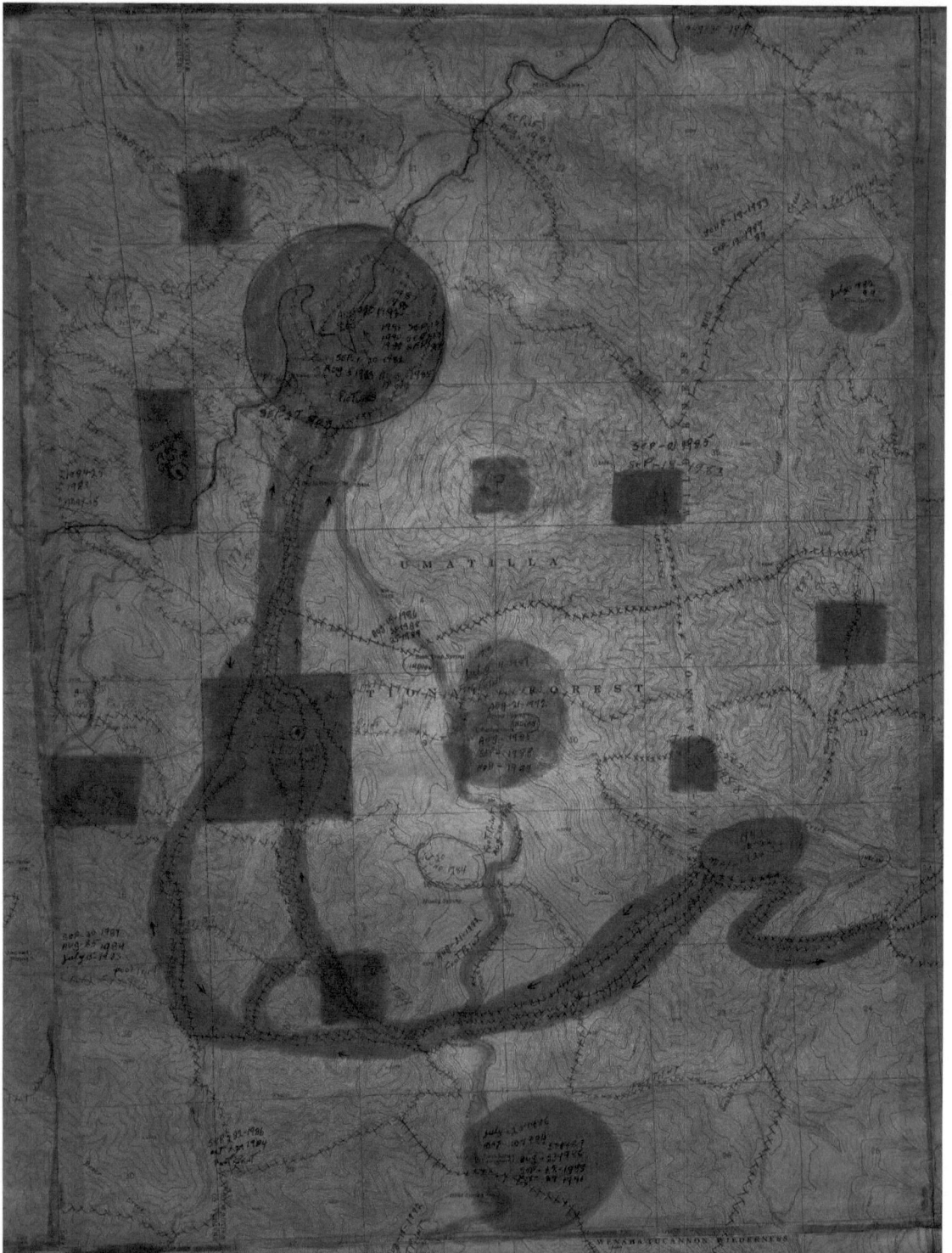

Freeman Map individual section view 5 - The large highlighted circle toward the top shows the Deduct Spring area. Notice the immense amount of activity recorded here over the years.

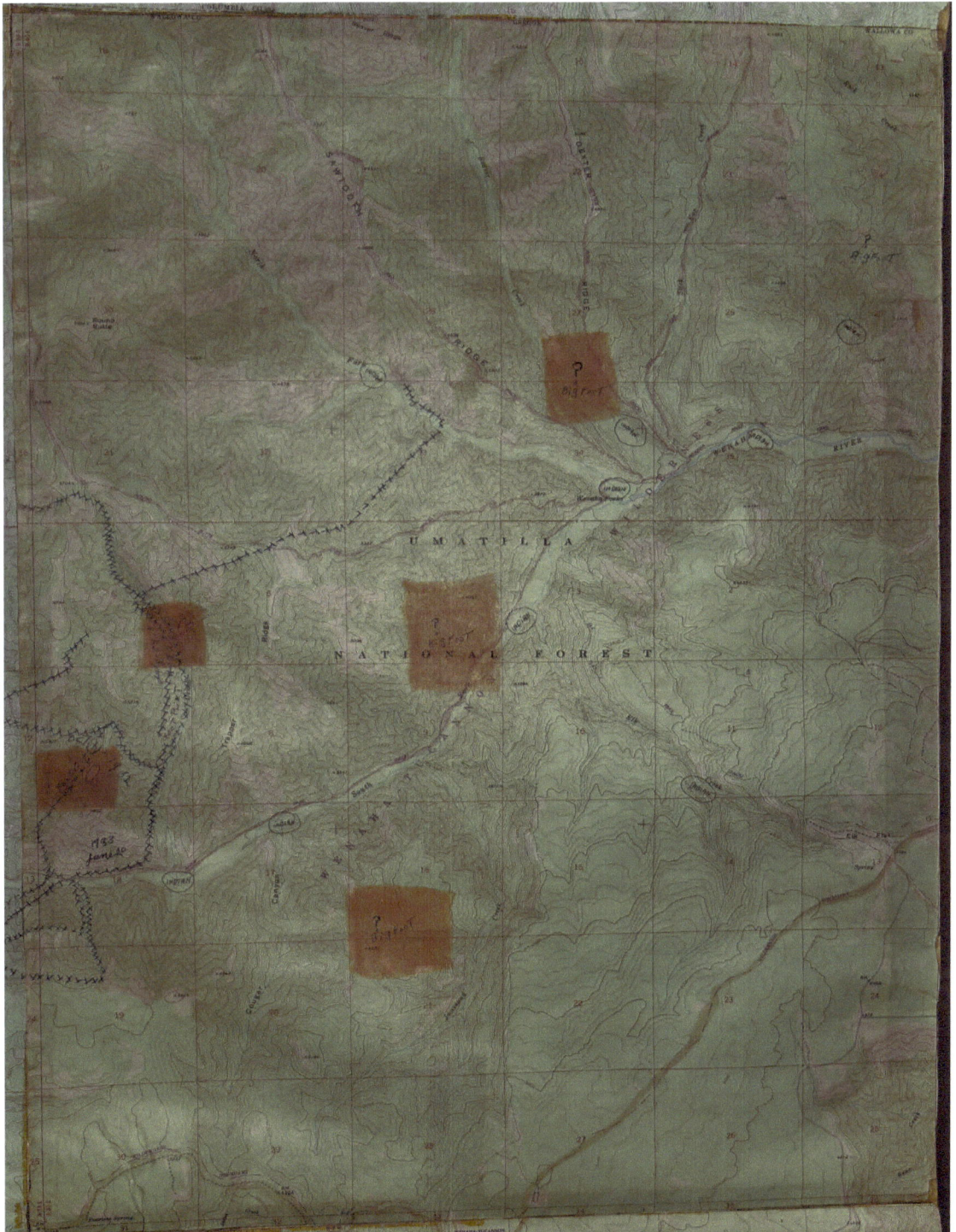

Freeman Map individual section view 6 - The question marks seen on the map represent possible areas where Freeman thought the creatures could be nesting or "wintering". Unfortunately, these are not places you can access, or would want to try to access during the winter.

Freeman Map individual section view 7 - Circles with the word "Indian" inside of them represent areas that were thought to have been used by Native Americans. Some artifacts including arrowheads were discovered at one or more of these locations.

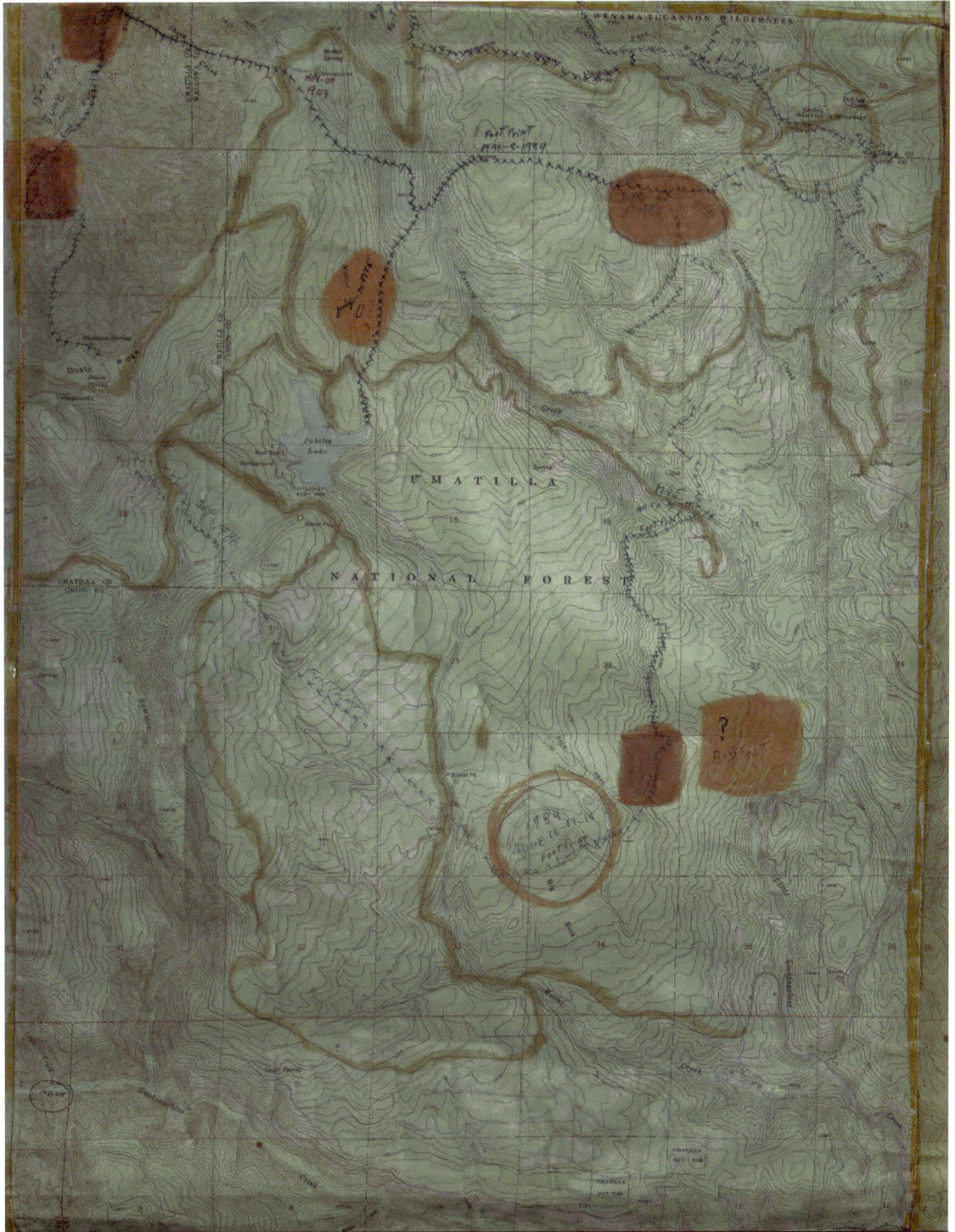

Freeman Map individual section view 8 - There is a large highlighted section and a date of June 15, 1983, here, but no other information aside from the intersecting trackways of why this area was highlighted. Perhaps it was another type of encounter such as vocalization, but at this time I do not know.

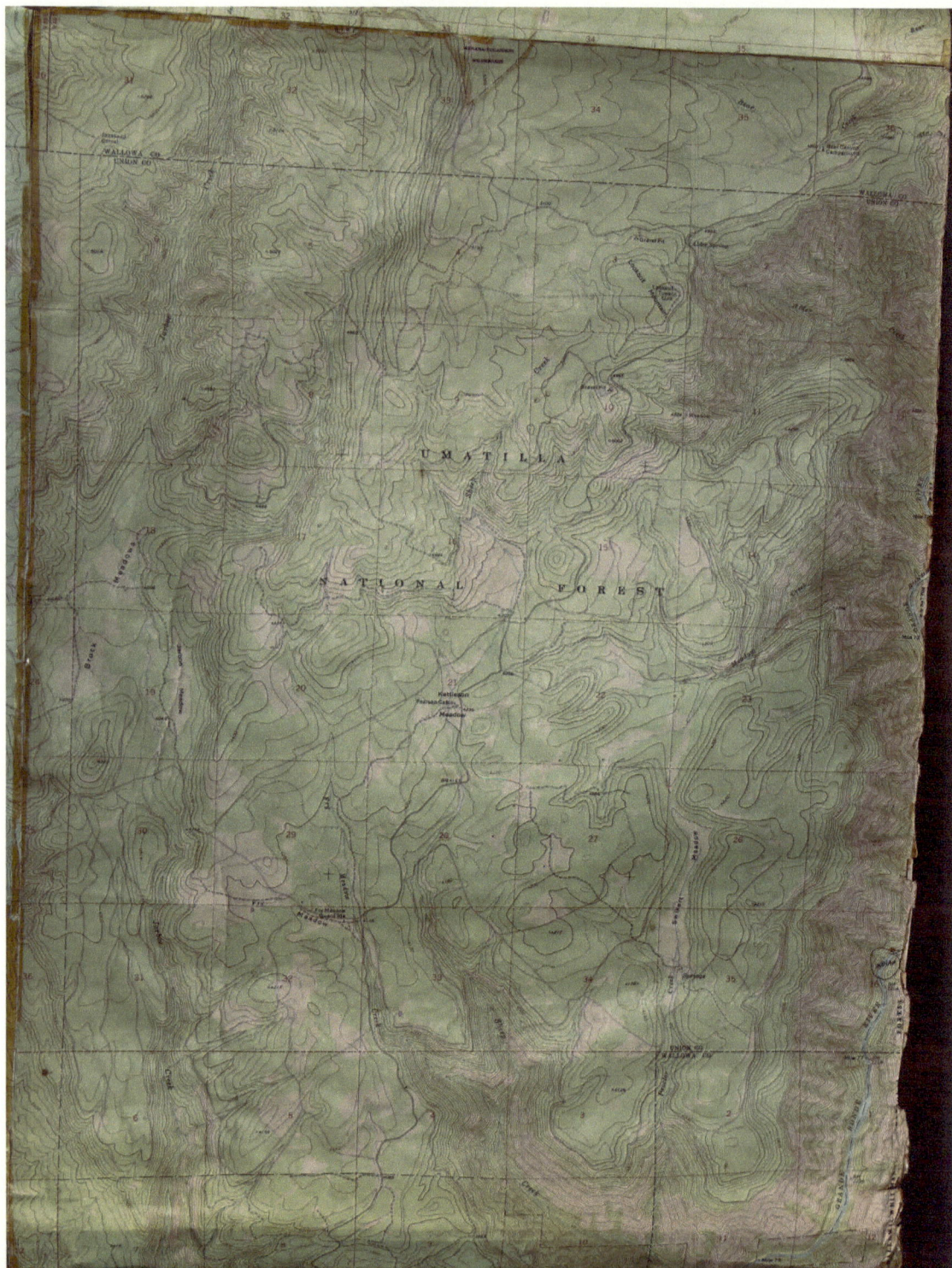

Freeman Map individual section view 9 - This section is all but undocumented with the exception of one "Indian" marking to the southeast along the Grande Ronde River.

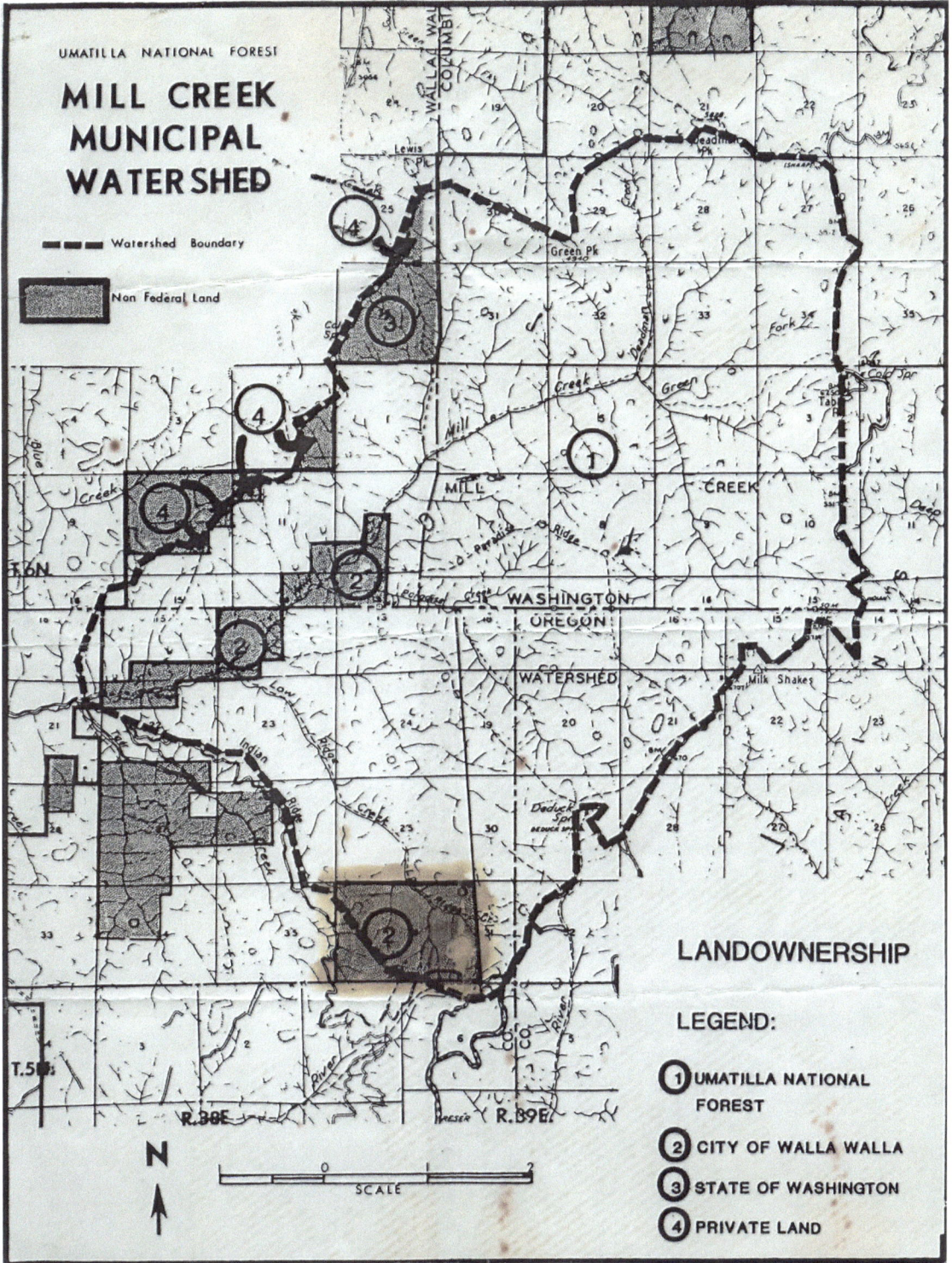

A map of the Umatilla National Forest Mill Creek Municipal Watershed Landownership.

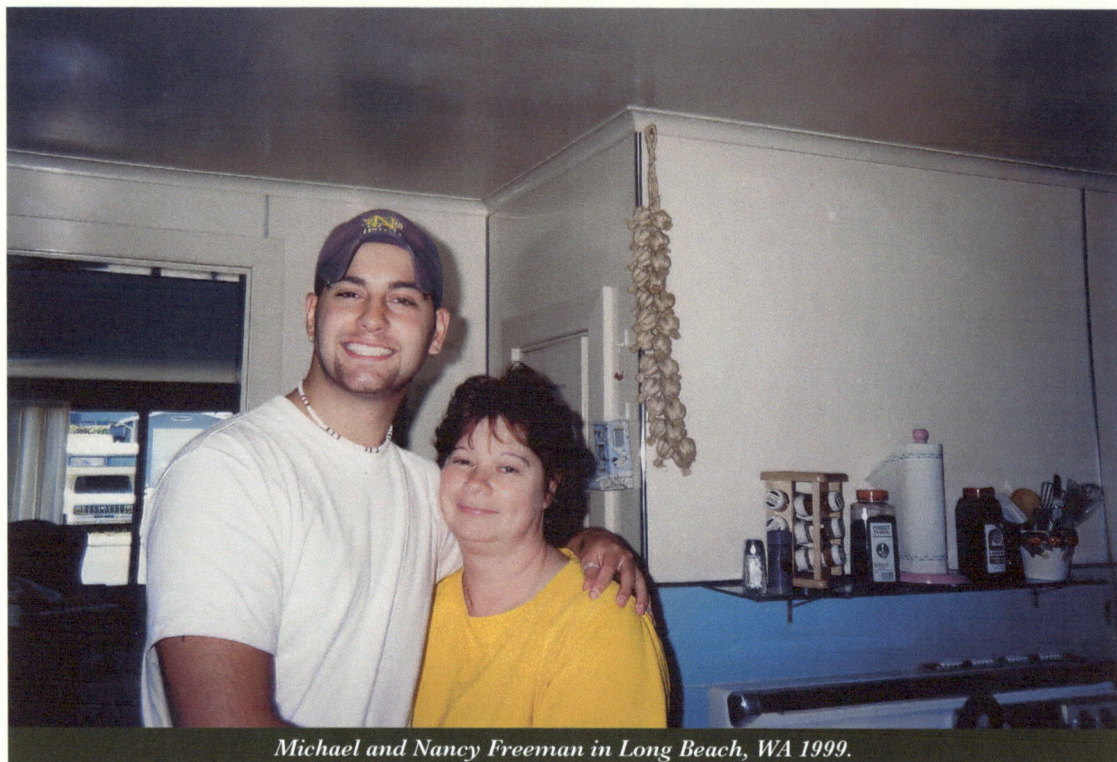

Michael and Nancy Freeman in Long Beach, WA 1999.

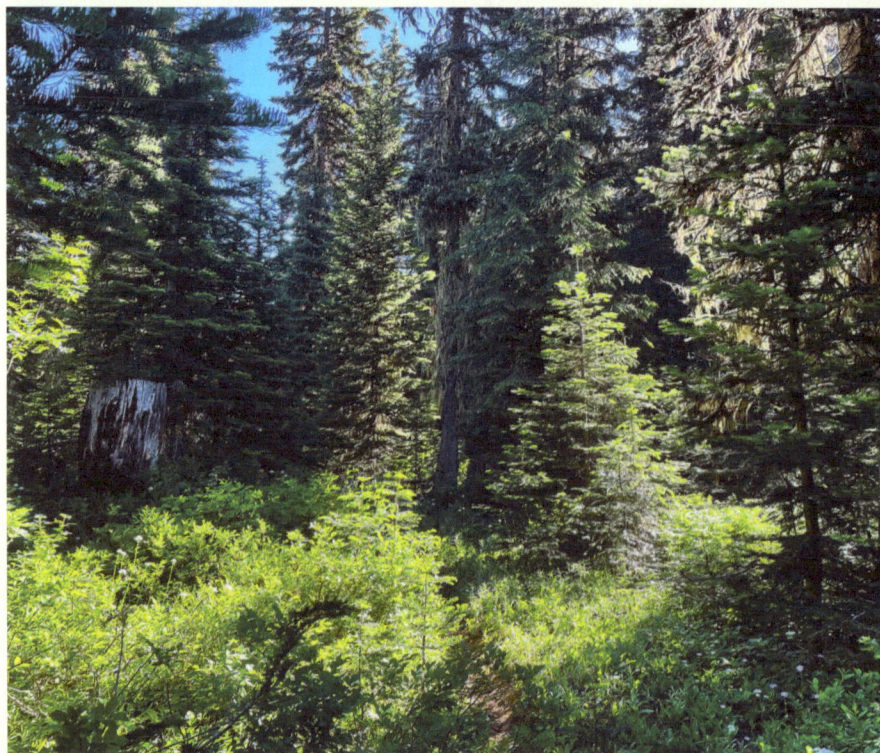

The Deduct Spring footage site as it looks today. Although the tree the creature brushes past in the footage is much larger now, it is clearly recognizable. This photo was taken on July 20, 2022, by Cliff Barackman.

David Been and Cliff Barackman at Dave's home in 2017. Photo courtesy of Cliff Barackman.

3.

THOUGHTS ON THE BLUE MOUNTAIN EVIDENCE

Cliff Barackman

My first introduction to Paul Freeman's sasquatch evidence was in the early 1990s through Dr. Grover Krantz's book, *Big Footprints* (later retitled *Bigfoot/ Sasquatch Evidence* in its second edition). He was mentioned by name several times in the book, and elsewhere referred to as a "forest service employee." It was clear that Freeman had collected important footprint casts, but at the time of the book's publishing (1992), he was only halfway through his bigfooting career. By the time of Freeman's death in 2003, he and his network of researchers would have gone on to collect one of the largest bodies of physical evidence supporting the existence of sasquatches.

Like any high-profile bigfoot researcher, Freeman had issues with the community and the media. Even today, some accuse the man posthumously of being a hoaxer, and even an admitted hoaxer. They point to an interview with Freeman on *Good Morning America* in which he states that he made fake footprints but ignore the context of him doing this as an experiment to find out how hard it would be to fake the kinds of footprints he was finding. Any bigfoot researcher who is interested in footprints and castings would do this same thing. I have done this, as have many others.

Others say that Freeman had to have hoaxed evidence because there was so much of it coming out of the Blue Mountains during this time. This argument ignores several important facts. First, Freeman was an excellent tracker having grown up in Iowa and the woods of Missouri. According to Freeman's son, there were times when Paul's hunting, tracking, and trapping skills literally fed the family. Paul Freeman was the sort of person that would find animal signs that others would simply not see.

Another fact ignored by Freeman's accusers is that the Blue Mountain evidence was not solely collected by Paul Freeman. There was a network of well-connected researchers sharing their information and resources to follow up on as many sightings, footprint finds, and rumors as possible. These other researchers included hobbyists, professional outdoorsmen, and professional man-trackers. As Freeman and the others became known as the go-to bigfoot people in the Walla Walla area, more information found its way to their ears and was shared accordingly. When Freeman or anybody in his network would follow up on a story, they would usually cast any footprint evidence that they found at the site, real or not. This introduced some fake footprints into the Blue Mountain evidence, but the researchers themselves were not the source of the hoaxed material. They were just documenting what they found as any good researcher would do. And finally, Freeman and the others were simply out in the woods a lot. For some of them, it was a sort of obsession, and for others, it was their job as professional trackers, packers, and biologists. One does not find bigfoot footprints by sitting behind a computer in the big city, after all.

Ironically, the reasons that Freeman gets accused of hoaxing are all attributes of a good bigfoot researcher: tracking skills, time in the woods, experiments with hoaxing techniques, and having a close-knit network of other enthusiasts with whom information is shared.

The Blue Mountain evidence increased the data set of footprint and handprint casts dramatically. Much of what has been observed in the foot and hand casts has been found to be consistent when compared to other casts taken by other people in other places and times. Take for example the footprint cast from June 16, 1982, that Freeman obtained that showed the fat pad curve around a large rock. This cast suggested that the plantar pad in sasquatches was much thicker than in humans, which would have been a reasonable guess, to begin with. Six years later, Freeman cast another such print showing a large (2-inch square) rock embedded into the plantar surface of another foot. One can see the curve of the fat pad around the rock showing that the impression was not made by a rigid prosthetic foot. In 2013, hundreds of miles away in Humboldt County, CA, another sasquatch footprint was documented showing a large rock in the footprint around which the plantar pad had curved. I personally observed another example of this in the Southern California mountains back in 2008 when doing a follow-up investigation of some footprints adjacent to the San Gabriel Wilderness Area.

The thickness of the plantar pad was exhibited in another way as seen in a cast from Grays Harbor County, WA in 1982. In this case, the fat pad on the bottom of the foot expanded laterally into the substrate as the creature pressed down with the foot. As the creature's weight was lifted, the fat pad contracted back to its normal size leaving a concavity to the sides of the footprint wall. This is called the "mushroom effect," as coined by Dr. Krantz. This same feature can be observed in several casts collected by Freeman, but most notably in the "Wrinkle Foot" casts from Table Springs near the Walla Walla River. Once again, the large data set showed other examples of interesting features from other casts collected elsewhere by others.

In June of 1982, Freeman cast a set of footprints in such a fine substrate that skin ridge detail, like fingerprints, showed on various locations of the casts. These skin ridge details are known as dermatoglyphics. Over the next few years, several more casts showing dermatoglyphics were found and cast by Freeman. We can find other examples of casts taken by other people in other parts of the continent that show these same features. Several casts from Kentucky show clear dermatoglyphics.

Sasquatch handprints are rare, but there have been several examples collected by Freeman and others from the Blue Mountains. Before the first handprint evidence was obtained by Freeman in 1982, there were only two other casts and one tracing in the data set. The tracing, as documented by Chuck Edmonds in 1962, shows short, wide fingers with an extensive palmar surface (likely the result of extended webbing between the fingers) and a strange thumb position. Eight years later in 1970, two hand casts from northeastern Washington showed the same features, but with more details than a tracing could show indicating that the thumb was not opposed in the same way as a human thumb, but rather rotated so that it could flex more in line with the other fingers. Another feature noted was the lack of a robust thenar eminence, the protrusion at the base of a human thumb where muscles that help control the thumb are located. These same features would later be verified by handprint examples from the Blue Mountain data set, as we will see.

In 1982, a knuckle impression was cast by Freeman in an elk wallow near Tiger Saddle in the Blues. Extending out from the curled knuckles was a thumb that showed the thumbnail position on the back of the creature's thumb. If this hand was to open rather than being flexed into a fist, the thumb would be in the same position as what was interpreted in the two hand casts from 1970. Freeman would go on to cast several more handprints, and all of them show this feature. In 2014, 2016, and 2021, handprints would be cast in northern Kentucky that all show this same thumb position, as well as the thick, short fingers and lack of thenar eminence.

Another noteworthy congruence that can be found in the Freeman footprint casts is evidence of the midfoot flexibility of the sasquatch foot inferred by the location of the pressure ridge raised upon push-off of the foot. While Krantz noted in 1992 the "considerable internal flexibility" of the sasquatch foot, Dr. Jeff Meldrum was the person who elaborated on the location of this flexibility: the midtarsal joint. Meldrum published the information in 1999 and shed light upon features seen in casts dating back to 1958. Many of the Freeman casts show this same pressure ridge at exactly the position predicted by Meldrum's assertion. Most of these casts were found before Meldrum published his work and was thus unknown to researchers.

The Blue Mountain bigfoot evidence gave us a reasonable sample size to compare other tracks against. Footprints and handprints found by other researchers in other states, both before and after the heyday of bigfooting in the Blues, continue to show features that can readily be observed in the Blue Mountain data set.

Sasquatches are obviously rare animals. It would therefore make sense that enough footprints found in the same general area over time would probably contain multiple footprints from the same individuals. A close inspection of the Freeman evidence combined with a familiarity with the sasquatch foot structure and flexibility yields many examples of the same individual sasquatch's footprints being found over many years. Only a large data set, such as what Freeman and the other researchers in the Blue Mountains left us, could offer the opportunity to see this.

While identifying individual animals by their footprints involves some level of speculation, what becomes very clear in this exercise is some notion of their range and population size. Early results from mapping footprint finds from the Blues and elsewhere indicate that these animals have a low population and don't range as widely as some have hypothesized over the years. Freeman himself started the data gathering of track finds and sighting reports on his personal research map, which now hangs in the North American Bigfoot Center. By connecting the dates and locations on the map with individual footprints, we can see the movement of individuals over time. Perhaps this will eventually lead to understanding why the animals went to these spots at that time of year, which might eventually lead to intercepting an animal as Freeman did at Deduct Springs in August 1992. Paul used his map and data to drive his research.

Freeman and the rest of his Blue Mountain network of researchers have passed onto us a tremendous body of evidence with which we can compare other finds. It takes a large data set to be able to make generalizations, and even today we are just getting to the point where there are enough casts to do this. Like the pioneers of bigfoot research back in the 1950s and 60s, Freeman and the others in his circle have laid a foundation on which we can continue to build our knowledge.

Lateral view of the embedded rock.

"Rockfoot" found and cast on September 29, 1988. You can see in the track that this animal stepped directly on a large rock, forcing it both down and forward into the ground.

This photo of Rockfoot shows the track after the rock had been removed. There is at least one contributor to this book that believes there is a possibility that this cast may indeed belong to Wrinkle Foot, and the immense size of the track is due to the foot sliding. Look at the toes here and compare them to other Wrinkle Foot casts. Do you agree?

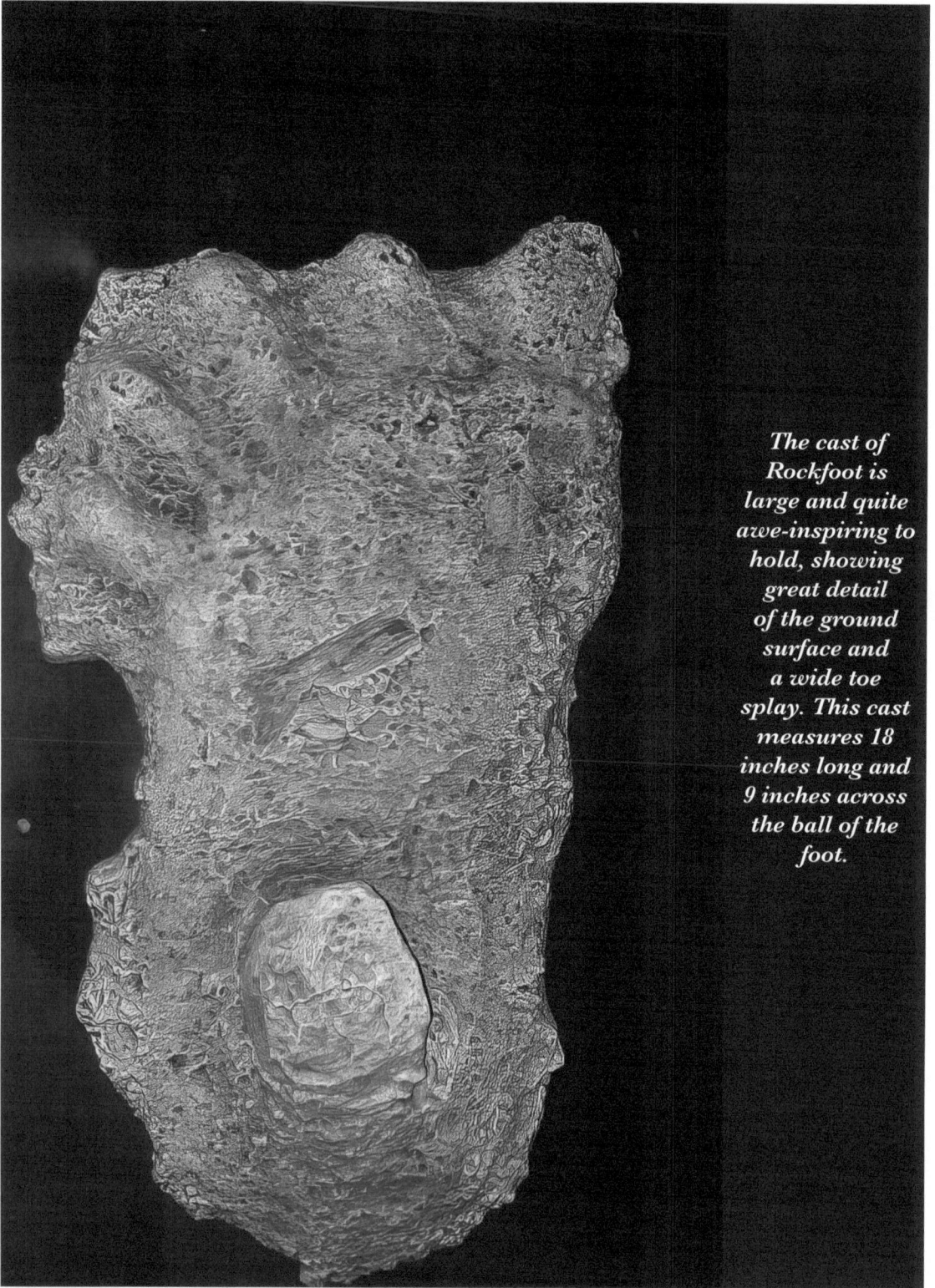

The cast of Rockfoot is large and quite awe-inspiring to hold, showing great detail of the ground surface and a wide toe splay. This cast measures 18 inches long and 9 inches across the ball of the foot.

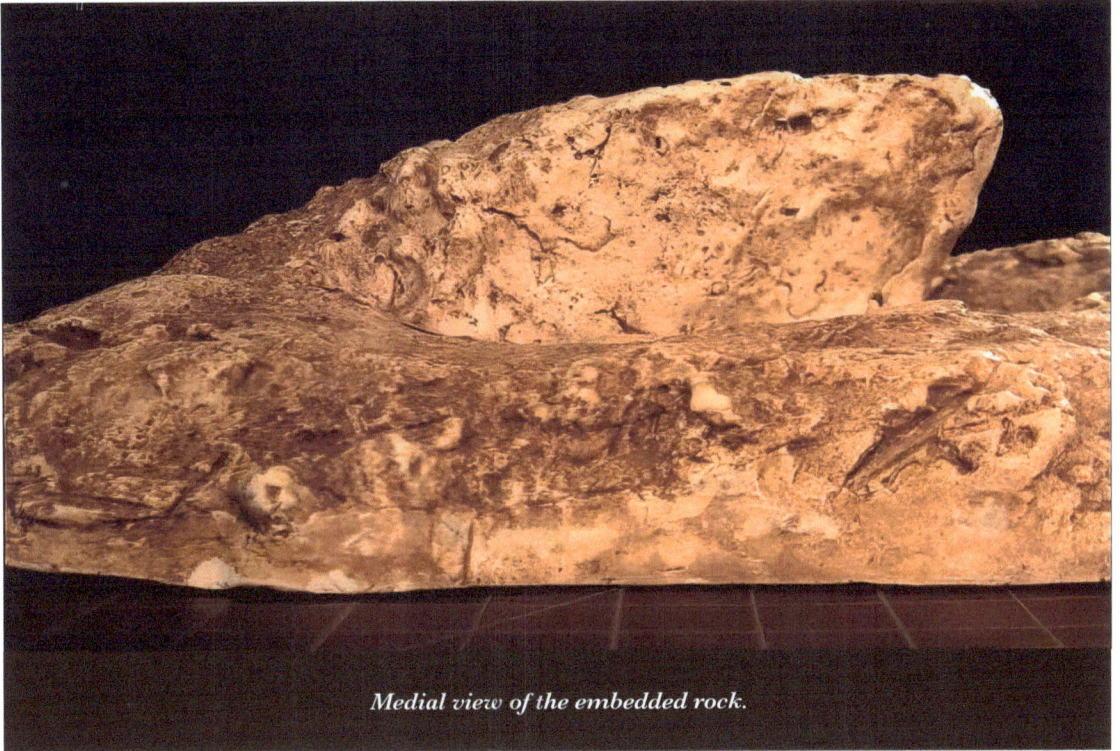

Medial view of the embedded rock.

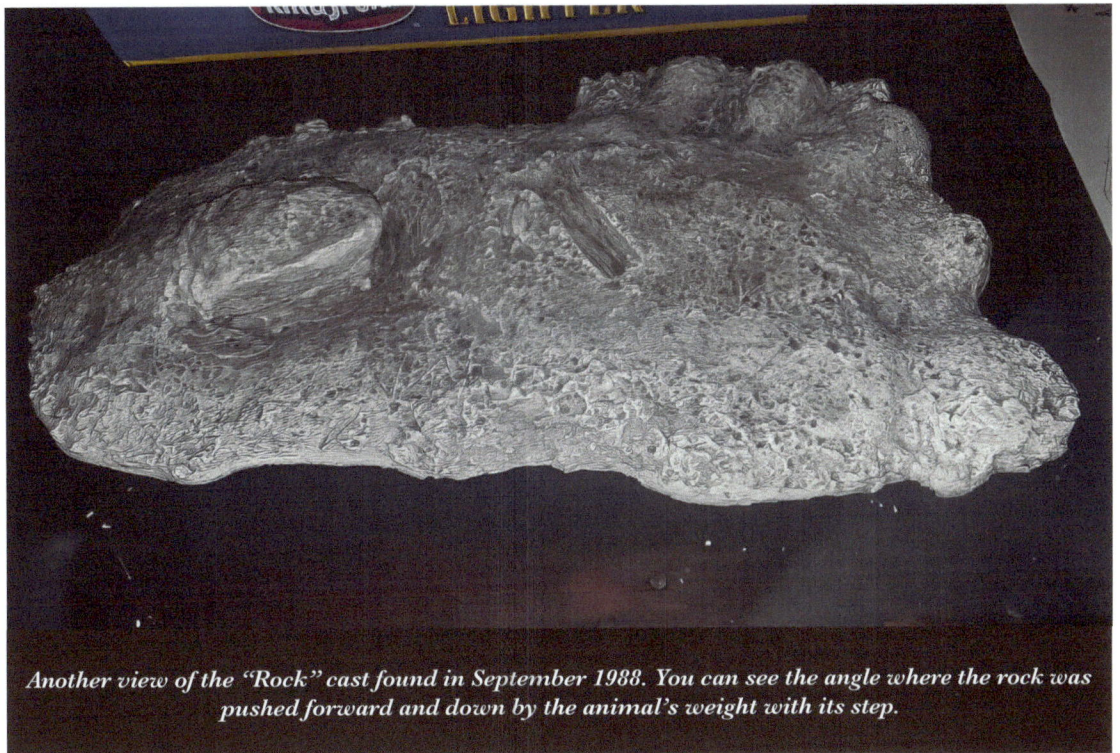

Another view of the "Rock" cast found in September 1988. You can see the angle where the rock was pushed forward and down by the animal's weight with its step.

A photo of the Rockfoot cast without the rock.

4.

BLUE MOUNTAIN LEGACIES

Johnathan C Sumerlin

I didn't know Paul Freeman as well as most people. I grew up the grandson of another legendary Bigfoot researcher, Wes Sumerlin. To be completely honest growing up I was not a solid believer in Bigfoot. I looked at the subject more as a ghost story that you told around the campfire. On several occasions, grandpa and many other local legends in the Bigfoot research community would meet at the Blue Mountain mall in Walla Walla Washington. Most Sundays, you could find my grandpa, Paul Freeman, Bill Laughrey, occasionally Grover Krantz, Vance Orchard and I believe David Been showed up a few times. I actually nicknamed this group the Blue Mountain Bigfoot research organization which is the group I started many years later with the next generation of Bigfoot researchers. Those Sundays were usually very interesting. They would get together to show off tracks that had been found, talk about reports that were made and general plans of where they wanted to travel in the blue mountains. All of them had extensive experience in the blue mountains with either the forestry service or working with the forestry service in various areas of expertise.

Now since this book is about Paul, I honestly can't say that I really knew him that well. Back in those days, kids were meant to be kind of seen, definitely not heard. I would listen to Grandpa and Bill and Paul tell stories about Bigfoot and the trackways they found or the sightings they had. In fact, when Paul shot his video, that was actually not long after I became a believer. Yes, that's right, even though I am the grandson of Wes Sumerlin, I actually gave an interview to Vance Orchard saying that I think my grandpa fell off his horse one too many times. There wasn't no giant monkey running around the mountains.

That summer I was proven wrong, I was 14. I remember after I had my first sighting Grandpa had me tell about my encounter multiple times and a lot of times people didn't know what to think. Most people are either believers or they're skeptics - there wasn't a lot of middle ground. Paul was one of the first serious researchers I had a chance to tell my encounter story to and just like his video when I watched it the first time and asked 1 million questions, he asked me to repeat it, and then repeat it again and then again. We went over it, we discussed what most likely startled the Bigfoot to cause our encounter and it was the first time I think when dealing with Grandpa, Paul and their friends in the Bigfoot world at the time, that I was for even a moment looked upon as a fellow Bigfoot researcher and not just one of the kids. He showed me respect that I didn't expect to get.

After I had my first sighting and became a firm solid believer in the subject I wanted to learn everything I possibly could. I got my grandpa to start teaching me how to track and how to read trail. I got them to tell me all the stories again and this time I actually listened. When Paul showed up at the Sunday meet and greets or came over to Grandpa's house for coffee, I sat and listened to every word trying to learn everything I could. I remember when he showed up with the video he was in a very interesting mental condition, to say the least. I can't think of a good word to describe his mental attitude at the time so that's the best way I can explain it. He was excited that he got it on video but he was also kind of nervous, like, *holy crap this thing is around the mountains*. I think we watched that video so many times I thought we were going to wear it out. And since I was finally a believer, I was able to be heard and not just seen. I had all kinds of questions and then I watched the Patterson film. I actually seen Paul's video before I ever seen the other video.

It's uncanny how similar the two videos are over several hundred Miles and a couple of decades apart. This video was a true milestone for all the researchers in the area. It laid the foundation for future researchers to strive on and motivate us to keep going to find that new evidence. It was just the year before the Freeman video was taken I believe, that we had a track way found along Mill Creek that was 7 miles long.

This was one of the big first "expeditions" I guess you would call it that I got to work on with Paul and grandpa out in the field. I remember asking Paul and Grandpa, but mostly Paul how they can tell these were real tracks. Keep in mind anybody who knew Paul knows he was not a small man he was well insulated. So he went up next to one of the tracks in the track way, actually several, and stood next to it and actually kind of bounced a little bit next to the track and even as big as a man as he was he couldn't sink even close to what the tracks of the Bigfoot made. That's when he and Grandpa pointed out that if someone really wanted to fake a trackway nobody had the endurance and the size to make it 7 miles long. Somewhere in there would've been evidence showing that it was man-made, and there was nothing.

After that track way, occasionally grandpa Vance or Paul would get random reports from people and I actually got a call from Paul a couple of times asking me if I wanted to go check this out. He was busy doing something or other so it would be me and my dad going and we would ask questions and take interviews, get all the information, the location, etc. As much information as we can, and then would pass it on to Paul and Grandpa and everybody else. If we were able to, me and Dad would go look and see what we could find, and for the most part, we'd pass it off to Grandpa because even though I wanted to check out every report credible or otherwise, I still had to go to school on a daily basis. Plus around that time I started working weekends.

For the Walla Walla area, there are only a handful of researchers that I guess you would refer to as the forefathers of Bigfoot research for the Blue Mountains. Paul was by far one of them. He knew those mountains like the back of his hand and he was a very credible man. When the Good Morning America show came to town in 1987 and interviewed all of them about Bigfoot, one of the interviewers actually asked Paul if he had ever hoaxed or faked a track, and he said yes. What a lot of people don't realize is that the interview went on for a couple more minutes where he explained why he made fake tracks. It goes back to what I was saying earlier when we were walking along the track way and he stepped next to a Bigfoot track and still couldn't sink as far as the track head. He made fake tracks at home to study if it was possible to recreate a track using human man-made power. But as interviews go, in many cases, the media will edit what they feel will increase their ratings even if it discredits those they are interviewing.

Soon after Paul's footage, we moved to Yakima, and then shortly after that following graduation, I moved to Spokane. My bigfoot research after that took a back burner to life, but I always kept my eyes open and listened to reports. In the back of my mind, even after Grandpa and Paul passed, I still sometimes ask myself how they would handle this particular report, what questions would they ask.

As long as there are Bigfoot reports or Bigfoot evidence being found especially in the Blue Mountains, Paul Freeman will always be remembered as one of the forefathers of Blue Mountain Bigfoot research. He and the other legends in the area laid the foundation for those of us continuing to look for this elusive creature to stand on, and hopefully get a better point of view by learning from our past. We can ask the same questions they did, then use that foundation to develop our own and propel it to the future.

On a personal note, I just want to say thanks for all you did Paul, if it wasn't for you, my grandpa Wes Sumerlin, Grover Krantz, Bill Laughery, David Been, Vance Orchard and many others, those of us continuing your legacies Wouldn't be as equipped as we are to continue looking for "Big Jim's" family.

Paul Freeman getting ready to cast a footprint near the water's edge at Deduct Spring, August 21st, 1992 just a day after he had captured video footage at this very site.

5.

THE FREEMAN FOOTAGE

August 20th, 1992
Deduct Spring, Oregon

Michael Freeman

It wasn't completely by chance. It wasn't completely by luck. And it wasn't completely due to research. I think it would be more accurate to say that it was a combination of the three. Ten years, two months and ten days after his initial encounter with a Sasquatch in 1982, Paul Freeman, with casting supplies, and his video camera in hand, found himself heading a little later than usual to a familiar spot in the Blue Mountains. Video footage was indeed intended to be filmed that day, let us be clear on that. But what exactly was filmed at Deduct Spring on August 20th, 1992 was not what Paul Freeman had in mind.

Deduct Stagecoach

Hot, dry summers are not unusual to the area, and that summer of 92' was no exception. Usable water sources were drying up by mid-August, and wild game was moving to viable sources that were still plentiful. Paul knew that Deduct Spring was one such resource, and had been visiting it for years in search of evidence around the water's edge. This particular August, Freeman had been there more than usual, as he was noticing more than usual activity, and in the week or so leading up to the 20th had already found footprints in the area along with some unusual disturbances along the banks of the spring pond. They were coming there, he was certain of that. And he was certain that they were doing so before sunrise, in the cool of the early morning, with the cover of darkness still providing protection.

My father, at the time, was working the night shift driving a truck at a plant for a waste disposal outfit. When his shift would end around four am. He would climb into his truck and make the drive into the Blues and to Deduct Spring. Often waiting in the shadows for the light to come, he would then make his rounds, checking for fresh footprints and any other signs of evidence that may point to the presence of Bigfoot. Tracks were often cast if found, and it wasn't uncommon for him to document this on video. I have hours of footage actually. Footage of him and some of the other old-timers investigating a trackway, casting footprints, or following broken tree branches. Often he would simply just scan the scenery and talk about the watershed. It was not uncommon for him at all, he did it quite often, and he had already been doing it at Deduct that summer. One day followed another, and the process was repeated, sometimes evidence was found, but there was always the lingering thought that he was missing them somehow. They had to be coming earlier than he was. They would have been used to him by now, at least to his scent. They would have known when he was present, they would get used to the time he was coming. Everything we think we know about bigfoot points to them being highly intelligent. Of course, they knew.

On the weekends, when my father wasn't working, he got out of bed and up to Deduct earlier than ever, and he had been there every day that week, watching. So you see, it wasn't just research that led to his footage being captured, and as I previously said it wasn't just luck either, there was a third element at play. My father was wrong about one thing, they were not coming earlier than he was and leaving, instead, they were watching and waiting for him to leave. But the element of chance was about to change everything.

Shortly before heading to work on the night of Wednesday, August 19th, 1992 my father received a telephone call from my sister, Linda. She was having difficulty trying to get her car to start and had called to see if dad would swing by and fix it for her. He agreed. So my father headed off to work that night with no plans of any sort to go to the mountains the next day. My father went to work that night with plans to come home for some much-needed rest and to a morning visit with my sister which would surely result in him having to repair something that could have easily been avoided with just a bit of care. My father kept his word. He finished work and went home. He slept. He got up on August 20th, 1992 and went to get a cup of coffee. He went to my sister's place and fixed her car. He got into his truck and started to head for home. And then he had a thought. "What the hell?" was the thought. "What the hell, I'll drive up there and just check." After all, maybe there would be fresh tracks worth casting. It was a beautiful, sunny day. Where else would he rather be anyway?

Paul Freeman walked right up on one. My father always believed the animal had just left the pond and was heading back up the trail when he startled it. One thing I'm certain about is that a mistake was made. A mistake was made by that animal that allowed him to get that close. It isn't one hundred percent certain if it stepped right out in front of him for distraction, to lead him away from something, or even to protect something, possibly a young one that was there as well. It is quite possible that all three of those things are the truth. But what we do know, what we know for certain, is that it chose to show itself to him. And it chose to look at him. And there is a reason for that. That I know is a certainty.

So you see, it wasn't just research, although there was plenty of that, ten years worth. He knew the area as well or better than anyone else. He knew the right spot. He knew the right reason. He knew they were there. There are researchers who spend their lives putting in the work and thinking that they know, just to never have a single encounter. And it wasn't just luck. No, not that, he was too well prepared. His first sighting in 1982, that was luck. When a nonbeliever sees one for the first time it certainly isn't research. That is luck. Luck and maybe a bit of something else. And it wasn't just chance. After all, he was right, there were tracks there to be cast. That's why he went, and that is why the camera was on. He was filming that set of tracks that ran down the road to the spring and back up again when he heard the brush start to pop. You see, he had the right spot. He had the right reason. He knew they were coming there. He knew he might find tracks, and he was doing what he always did. Chance is my sister's car not starting. Chance is him coming later than he normally would have. They were watching him, they were watching and they were waiting for him to leave. And when he wasn't there that morning, it made a mistake. It made a mistake and he walked right up on it.

That's Just What I'm Gonna Do

Of course, this isn't the end. Just as it wasn't the beginning. My father had spent ten years of his life tracking these animals, and by the time he started to move deeper into the forest an uneasy feeling was already set in. The moment he made a comment about there being more than one is the moment he started to worry. Excitement and shock were wearing off, and self-preservation was taking over. When you are dealing with a wild animal, and that one becomes two, the chance of the unknown happening multiplies exponentially. When that animal has a child with it, that unknown again multiplies drastically. That very thought was lingering in his mind, and the choice was made to remove himself from the situation. Did he pursue it? Yes, of course. Would he pursue it to no end? No, not when there were things waiting for him at home that were far more important.

My father may have had a few words for the man upstairs that day. He himself has said that a voice inside of him told him that maybe he better just leave them alone. Maybe enough was enough. Maybe he got as close as he was ever going to get and still be able to walk out of there and go home to his family. Paul Freeman chose to go home. The camera was shut down, and my dad proceeded to use a trail that he was familiar with to loop himself back around, trying to get to where he came in. He knew he was being watched and quite possibly even followed. They were still there, he could hear them. As my father would tell it, their vocalizations became aggressive and he feared for his safety. He came across a large hole in the ground where a tree had fallen and its roots had ripped out a large den underneath. My dad crawled down into the hole, underneath the shelter of the tree and roots, and waited for the threats to stop as he broke out into a cold sweat. He would later say that he has never been so scared in his entire life, and a period of time was spent cowering down like a frightened child. Once the screams and howls subsided his senses heightened, and the pace quickened. Paul used a ditch-like channel and crawled on his belly until he made it back to the pond. His aging and broken body did the best it could to get the hell out of there.

The next day he went back. With Wes Sumerlin and a small camera crew from the local news station at his side, he went back to cast tracks and look for any other physical evidence. A short news interview was given and tracks were found and cast around the water's edge. I've spoken some of beginnings and endings, and of this moment being neither. I suppose it could be seen as both his crescendo and at the same time his penultimate moment, as there wasn't much time left in either his research or his life.

You Would Too

Paul Freeman's career as an active Bigfoot researcher would last another five years. His life would last another ten. There were tracks found and casts made, but he never saw one again. August 20th, 1992 at Deduct Spring was his last sighting. Maybe that's because the research, and the luck, and the chance just never fell into place again. Or maybe that little voice inside of him, the one that was telling him maybe he should just leave them alone, would never allow himself to get that close again.

When it is all said and done what we are left with is an astonishing piece of visual evidence in support of the existence of Bigfoot. The Deduct Spring footage may not be as popular as that film from Bluff Creek in 1967 (you know the one I'm talking about), and that is just fine. After all, this is not a competition, but rather a collective effort that has spanned for decades. And that effort has continued to move forward as new generations of researchers armed with new technology are actively on the hunt. And it is hard not to think, what if? What if Paul Freeman had the advancements in the photo and video capabilities we have today? Would this mystery be solved? That is hard to answer, as there will always be someone who does not want to believe. Unfortunately we cannot turn back the clock, but what we can do, and what we are doing, is taking this new technology and applying it to what we already have. We are working with the newest technology to enhance my father's footage to the highest possible quality in order to be able to prove that there just might be a little more there than what most people realize. And when we do, we will present the best possible version of the Freeman Footage that the world has ever seen. And then maybe, just maybe, there will be a place on top of the mountain for my old man to sit.

Paul, with Wes Sumerlin next to him, pours casting material into footprints near the water's edge at Deduct Spring.

Adult tracks found around pond at Deduct Spring on August 21, 1992.

Wes Sumerlin can be seen standing with a small news crew who are interviewing Paul at Deduct Spring, near the site of his footage captured the day before on August 20th, 1992.

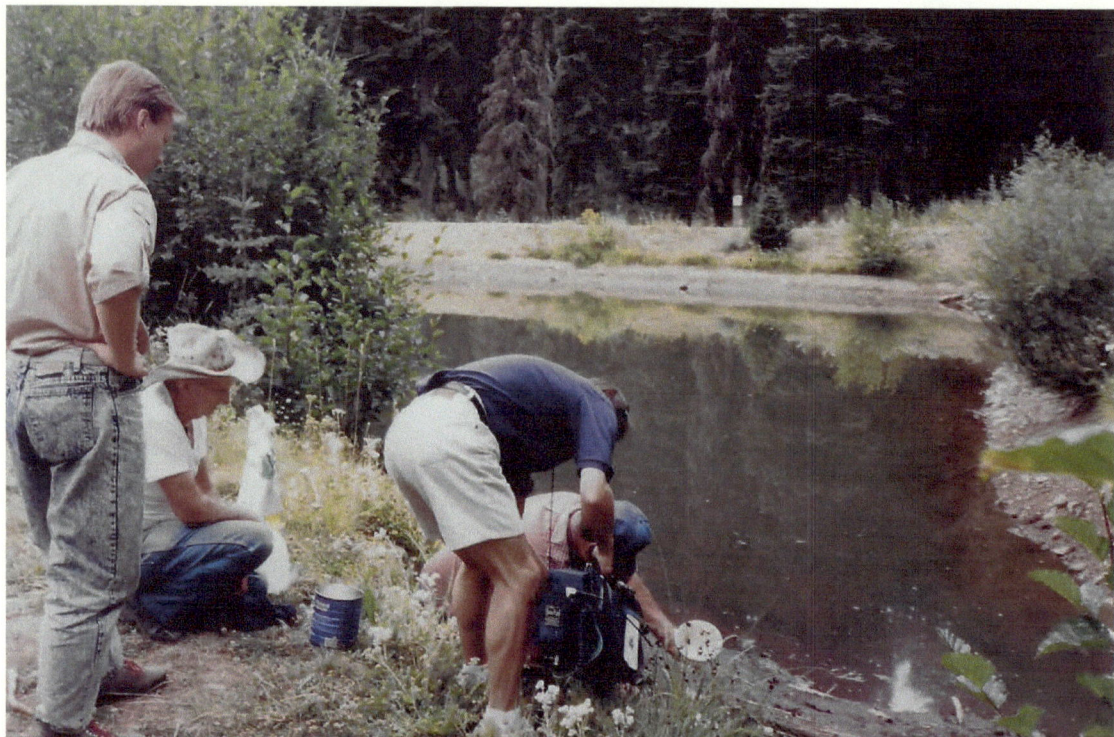

Paul showing the crew how to mix plaster for casting tracks at Deduct Spring on August 21, 1992.

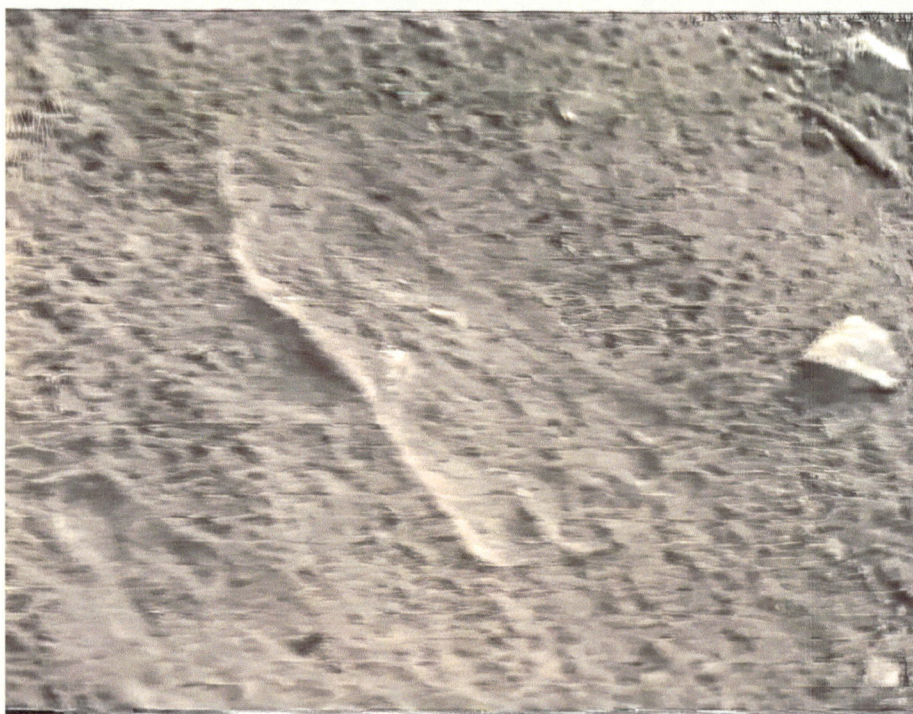

A still taken from Freeman's video at Deduct Spring on August 20, 1992, showing the footprints left at the site.

These stills from the video footage show the tracks Freeman was following that ran down the road to the spring pond, and then back up again to where the video was taken.

The tracks found at Deduct represent a known individual from the data set.

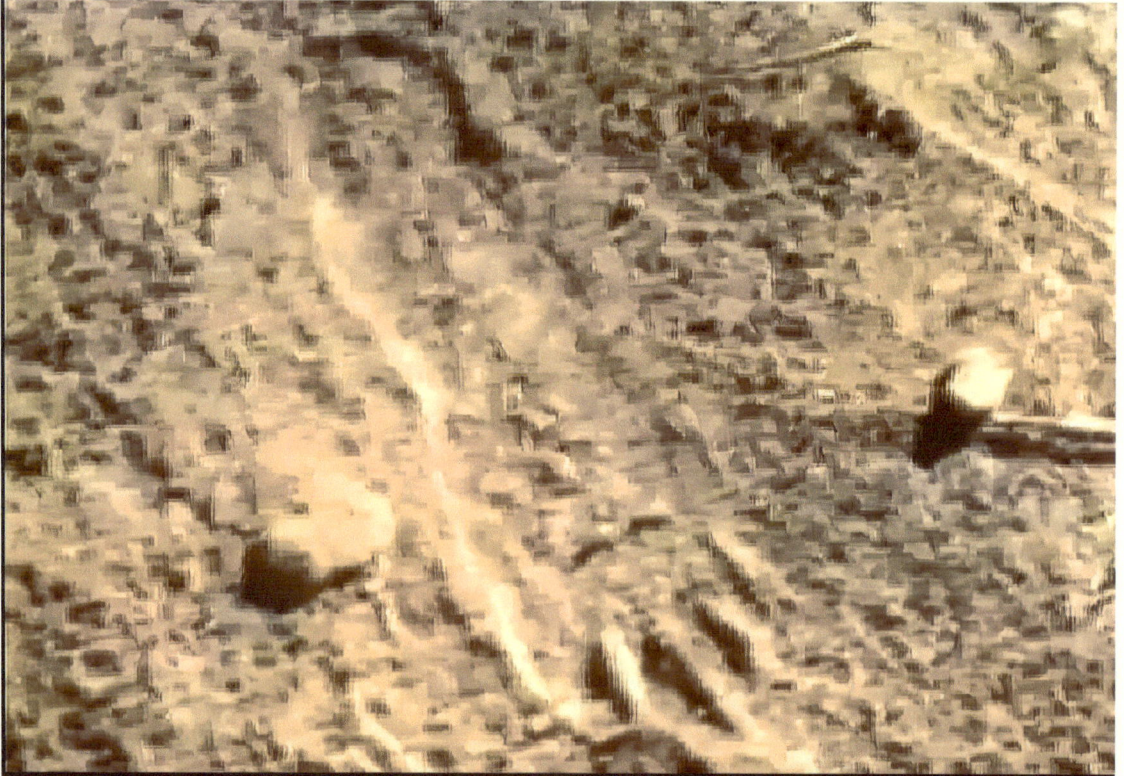

The individual from the Deduct tracks is thought to be the same individual that left tracks at both the 1991 Mill Creek Road Trackway and the 1996 5 Points Trackway.

These tracks are still being analyzed to ensure a positive identification match.

Two of the tracks found at Deduct Spring on August 21st.

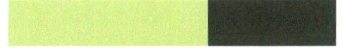

6.

EXPERT FOOTAGE ANALYSIS

Doug Hajicek

Throughout my time as a Sasquatch researcher, there have only been a handful of bigfoot films or videos that I felt were worth spending many hours analyzing. Jumping into the past, my many years of wildlife research, wildlife photography, and nature videography plus working with many field biologists and working closely with a handful of famed wildlife photographers had all taught me one important reality when I dove head first into the Sasquatch mystery. The one thing I badly needed was a critical eye when it came to alleged footage of the Sasquatch.

It was always either black and white for me: Fact or Faked…my 3-second rule. A rule that said don't waste time on this one or said you better dig way deeper. In other words, if the footage got past my natural skeptical instincts, I would be roped in and willing to devote personal time to learning all about the footage at hand. From the facts surrounding it to the environment to the filmmaker who supposably got the money shot. The camera used, the lens, the hows, and whys and what caused them to get lucky, what was different here, or was it just being at the right place right time by sheer accident?

It was indeed a very small ratio of films that were worth anything. Only about 1 in 20 passed that initial test for me. The 1967 Patterson Gimlin footage was one of them that passed initially along with every imaginable pace I could put the film through. This occurred even if it meant bringing other experts to weigh in such as Bill Munns, surgeons, bodybuilders, gait experts, scientists, anthropologists, or whomever I needed. It was a small number indeed, but a handful nonetheless. I looked for many tell-tale things almost instinctually. The flow of the creature, fluidity and graceful movement was one of the most important things I looked for. After all, if you watch tiger footage in a National Geographic doc, you know it's real immediately based on a million little details. Almost anyone would notice if it was a guy in a clumsy tiger suit or CGI animation, right? I concocted a list of other things that I would go through quickly if it made it past the first big barrier. A checklist of other details that my brain seemed to process faster if I just let it happen. Then I would methodically try to loop and FREL- Forward-Reverse enhanced loops to try to get details that most would miss by just watching it play through once or twice, plus put it on a good monitor of broadcast quality.

When I started the FREL process I usually was fairly convinced the footage was real or at least it had a good chance at being real, after all my time was and is valuable to me. None or an amount of limited red flags on the scorecard still would require serious attention and time. Devotion to perform more methodical stepped forensics that I did not take lightly, as I was often producing Bigfoot TV series – or documentaries like "Sasquatch-Legend Meets Science" or at least thinking about developing one. I did not ever want to promote hoaxed footage as likely being the real thing and I needed to up the odds that the footage would withstand the test of time and further future scrutiny from scientists. Here is the checklist summary and scoring system I computed in my head in a way that only the human brain can do using our complex intelligence. *Trust your gut instincts,* I often told myself. They never let me down even as a kid as I watched horror movies and TV shows in the 50s-60s and 70s. I wasn't scared because I knew it was fake and it looked fake. But it was the best we could do even with a big budget and teams of SFX, costume makers, and creative tricksters trying to scare the audience. So when I saw real unknown creatures like in the PG film, it was very different, my hair stood on end.

I was raised on fake crap, as so many of us were and your parents allowed you the freedom to stare at the countless horror and SciFi films that Hollywood cranked out. I could watch the creature from the black lagoon and feel zero fear because it just did not look real to me.

Again, an authentic piece of wildlife footage looks real at first glance! It will often withstand the test of time and future forensics. Also, I will say this with conviction: any Bigfoot footage will only have value if clear enough to see some damn details. *Please note: not all unreal Bigfoot footage is a purposeful hoax, but rather it may be just a misidentified object or animal.* This type of misidentified class of footage is the most common. It is vague, blobs of shadows obscured with leaves and branches seldom move and may as well just be a still photo. No time for this stuff in my research.

Valued Footage definition:

A) Most of the creature's body will show. A rare thing in Sasquatch film clips.

B) It will not be mostly obscured.

C) It will also offer real information on anatomy. Whether it be muscles, joint indexes, height, gait, weight and appearance. It should be illuminated enough for some unobstructed light to hit it. Anything less may have value to you, but has little value to science. Still photos must be sequential and clear also. "Blurry Blobs" that need a red circle to see it are pretty much non-counters.

D) You know instantly what a real Tiger is and when it is not CGI animation or a man in a suit. Use your instincts, chances are your first impression will be right. Your brain is hard to fool if you trust it.

1. **Anatomy.** Does it have stove pipe legs and arms? If so, give it... 3 Red Flags. The anatomy of any living mammal that is free of defined muscle and fat curves is probably not real... Game over right away!

2. **Is it a Lazy Hoax?** The Bigfoot in the clip has a high-contrast facial area just like the cheap costumes found on Amazon or Walmart. Because no effort was put in, give it 3 Red Flags. Facial areas, especially around the eyes and hairline will not look natural. An exaggerated look is often seen in commercial costumes.

3. **Bad acting.** Fakery in voice and mannerisms is seen and heard, also the audio may be missing, and most likely it was purposely removed. Please Add 1 Red Flag if the scene is overly set up, it most likely was staged. It's very difficult to fake a real event. Your instincts are very important here.

4. **Was it shot in the day or night?** The creature appears to have white hair and was taken with a game cam, security cam, or night vision camera using IR. So if the bigfoot is white, it isn't right. Add at least 1 Red Flag. Any IR lighting faux fur glows white due to the colored dyes used. Many clothes do the same thing.

5. **Hide a Seam.** Long hair on advanced costumes is always seen on shoulders to hide the removable head seam. Any seams seen on arms or legs or the backside between the shoulder blades are also a big nope, add 1-2 Red Flags. Costumes always have to be entered by the human prankster somehow. Also, look for any wrinkles or folds.

6. **Bell Bottom Britches.** If the film subject has wide ankles or a bell bottom-style costume that gets wider near the foot, it's fake. It is not natural anatomy for any biped. Ankles always narrow before it connects with the foot. Add 3 Red Flags. Wide costume construction near the foot is used to hide shoes.

7. **Timing.** The camera operator stopped filming for no reason when things just started getting good. Add 1 Red Flag. Or perhaps they started filming nothing special and a Bigfoot suddenly walks through the scene.

8. **Animation.** Decent CG animation hasn't been along much earlier than the mid-1990s, so jitter from animation is still pretty easy to spot. After all, you notice it in movies when they show an animated animal or person! If you think it could be animation chances, are it is. Add 3 Red Flags. Often coupled with too-good-to-be-true footage with no context or audio is a bad sign, making it as fake as a 3-dollar bill.

9. **I Just Filmed a Bigfoot.** The film's owner sought no experts, like myself, scientists or experienced researchers, or critical groups like the BFRO to examine it before showing it to the World. Add 1 Red Flag. It went straight to the Internet, often just playing on your curiosity to get views.

10. **It's All In The Eyes.** The face is not shown. Also, dead-looking eyes with no reflection or highlights or what could be just eye peek holes. Eyes are complex! Add 1 Red Flag. The face is the most complex thing a hoaxer can create, and it's why in most fake Bigfoot films the creature will never look at the camera, how convenient.

11. **Other Important Misc.** Scoring Measures Plus and Minus.

    a. No Footprint castings - add 1/2 Red Flag
    b. Past Hoaxes add - 3 Red Flags
    c. No other witnesses - add 1/2 Red Flag
    d. In an area where past sightings have occurred, remove 1 Flag
    e. Multiple witnesses - remove 1 Red Flag
    f. No name is connected to the footage - add 1 Red Flag
    g. The Filmmaker provided other types of accepted evidence – remove 1 Red Flag
    h. The proportions are larger than a human - remove 1 Red Flag.
    i. Subject has massive wide shoulders - remove 1/2 Red Flags
    j. The footage is too close up and unnatural looking - add 3 Red Flags.

12. **The Final Score, Score.** Your Favorite Bigfoot Footage scores as follows:

RED FLAG TOTAL

SCORING MAP

Red Flag sub total 0 - 1 Red Flags: Excellent Chance It's Real

Red Flag sub total 1 - 2 Red Flags: Very Good Chance It's Real

Red Flag sub total 3 - 4 Red Flags: Not Much Chance It's Real

Red Flag sub total 4 - 5 Red Flags: Almost Zero Chance It's Real

Red Flag sub total 6 - 10 Red Flags: Zero Chance It's Real

So, this is a good time to discuss the scoring of the Freeman footage, yes indeed. I remember well the day I first saw the footage and heard about it. Matt Moneymaker suggested I look at this footage that apparently met his personal criteria. Matt then put me in touch with Paul directly and it wasn't long after I had the original 8mm tape in my hand or a lossless digital copy.

I popped it into my professional Hi deck that could play both Hi-8 or 8 mm tape. I hit the play button and immediately thought, *wow*. The breathless sincere audio of Paul set off no Red Flags. Then I saw the lumbering slow walking creature step out from near invisibility in the full sun on the trees and the creature. Instantly, I noticed the hair and almost as fast, I saw what I describe as natural hair. From the color to the sheen, it was dead on for being real in my critical thoughts…

But that still did not rule out a suit made with animal hide. I was for sure waiting to be let down. Then I noticed the incredibly fast head snap the creature used to glance at the man holding the camera. It was that head snap that gave me my first chill, a chill that went deep. Next a bit more subtle, but nonetheless odd, I saw the creature seemingly grab a pine branch behind itself in what looked like an action to stop it from snapping or slow its swing down, something an animal would by instinct do if it traversed in the forest as it hunted or just wanted to cause a bit less disturbance.

Doing such an action behind itself blindly caused me to get a secondary chill and to make a note to myself to study that further. This was not something a man in a suit would or could do I thought. Then it stopped dead in its tracks, just behind small trees as if to stare at Paul for 2 seconds through the screen the young trees that offered some camouflage. It wasn't moving but blended in perfectly, something faux fur cannot and would not do. I was impressed so far, my instincts said yes, it's more than likely real… No Red Flags reared their ugly heads. Wow.

I also took note of the distended stomach, it also looked natural and yet out of place for any costume. It certainly was something I had never seen before in a supposed bigfoot clip. I thought this may be an older male and like us, it's a combo of fat and the hated furniture disease where one's chest falls into your drawers, something that happens to most male humans as we age.

Since it passed the first 2 phases of authentication more work was going to happen. The only red flag I gave it was 1 unofficial flag for wondering why was Paul talking at all…? His audio was very authentic and had no tell signs of acting, his words were clearly spontaneous, but the "why" bugged me a little bit. I cleared that question up after I got to know Paul, he just liked talking…a lot- period. Plus he was nervous and I think his own voice comforted him on some level. Paul was just one of those guys that had an open-book type personality if you know what I mean. He just didn't hide anything, spoke his mind with that bold but humble personality that was always kind, fair and confident.

THE SCORE

So my score on flags for Freeman's footage, like the PG film was simply zero in the end after hundreds of hours of study. In fact, when you get to the end of this chapter it has less than zero red flags if that's even possible. You may agree. You need to be your own judge, and I do think it's very important you form an educated opinion on both this footage and the mystery at hand in general. This mystery isn't going away…ever. It's fueled each day by good folks just going about their business. They see a Sasquatch cross in front of the car, lit brightly by the headlights and they don't need you telling them they are crazy or unobservant.

Please look at the facts and the evidence thoroughly… I mean in total… don't cherry-pick evidence. Look at all of it… listen to hundreds of eyewitnesses out of the 10k available to you, get educated on the hair, get informed on the hundreds of foot casts and why they are not easy to fake and what makes them different. Research anatomy, study this footage and the PG footage, look at the fingerprints, get familiar with important things like the IM index of the human body and then make a damn conclusion and not before. Get involved or button it up. Nothing worse than an ignorant opinion, really!

Keep in mind, other than talking with Paul Freeman by landline at the time, I knew nothing, zip of the area details, zero about why he was at that spot, and total ignorance about the geography nor the history of the area. After all, I had never even been to Washington state just yet either, I was from Minnesota. I was judging the footage on the footage and nothing else. This is always key at some point. It's the way I like it at least in the very beginning.

I called Matt and told him my initial thoughts and asked him a bunch of questions, Matt did have the majority of the answers and the story summary he told me of the spring at the film site that was located in the arid Blue Mountains immediately struck a chord with me. Water was one thing I did know of the Bigfoot sighting commonalities, it's that water was almost always a factor. Things started to make sense, and the more I learned about the circumstances and about Paul's research dedication, his job description, the more this unique footage just made sense. A forest serviceman who was highly experienced as a hunter and outdoorsman, who found bigfoot tracks at a clean, rare, yet plentiful water source in the vast semi-arid wilderness near a mountain peak. Water explained the researcher pinpointing the location to look for tracks and evidence. It just all made sense to me.

As a veteran wildlife filmmaker, I gathered the knowledge and awareness of living creatures to be able to study Bigfoot clips from more of a primordial point of view. That point of view was coupled with common sense about costume construction, basic anatomy, and lighting on fur and hair and this education helped me make solid conclusions on the authenticity of the occasional bigfoot footage that came to my production office.

My editing and computer experience helped with the variety of technical skills needed to be able to observe the footage in new forensic ways. Don't forget that I had the passion as I also once found huge tracks near water in the Arctic. In addition, I had several years being a professional investigator who worked downtown as they say, on a variety of tough cases that were now under my belt and had a better-trained sense of people, acting, lying and subtle nervousness, etc. All in all, I have a decent combo of skills that are needed for separating BS from the truth when examining supposed Sasquatch footage.

Any Sasquatch footage must stand on its own 2 feet (no pun) and survive a variety of Red Flag tests that are briefly outlined above. Taking each section of footage and using various contrast, zoom and looping effects, I broke the footage into sections to study. It was on the last section that I separated out, where Paul's audio is saying "there are two of them...." At this time, I knew he was most likely referring to the fact that he thought there were 2 adults as the one he filmed briefly and I presumed and heard that he had lost track of them.

In this clip, there was not much to see in the deep black forest shadows of the grainy shaky footage, but he saw something with his eyes that his consumer-grade camera did not see much of what his eyes did. This was just my opinion. But, I did not give up trying to understand what was in this clip. Then all of a sudden after looping it extensively, I noticed an abnormality in the footage that seemed to be moving like a hinged elbow, but it was too small and thin to be any part of any bigfoot anatomy. What the heck was I looking at?

I continued to watch the loop where the last frame started the loop backward, a very smooth way to observe movements. Then I noticed a second appendage, this puzzled me only for a few seconds longer until a theory had it hit me…is this a baby being lifted?

I ran upstairs and lifted my young 2-year-old up from the floor where she was playing and low and behold, I observed first-hand the exact leg clawing motion from her young legs to try to help her walk-grip-claw up dad's body to get as high as she could. I put her down with a kiss and sprinted back down to my studio monitor to watch again and again and again…I was maybe, and likely, observing a baby sasquatch being lifted by a parent and that just maybe the distended stomach was that of a postpartum female sasquatch who was possibly intentionally leading Paul away from the infant.

Next, I looked for a small head and yes when the contrast was lightened on my monitor it was there deep in the shadows. Subtle but it was there. Ok then maybe it is a Sasquatch infant? This inferred conclusion just felt right to me, it checks all the boxes.

I am not sure who I called first, Matt Moneymaker or Paul Freeman, as I only distinctly remember my conversation with Paul, plus his amazing reaction to the news and theory. I must have also had a bit of overexcitement in my voice when I explained what he may have captured. After all, I pretty much knew what it wasn't and it left little room for what it was.

He just said, "Oh my God Doug, really, really, this is good news."

I said, "It really seems amazing. I for the life of me, cannot think of any other thing it could be as the small appendages are articulating on their own and where a small head should be if it's a baby, also rises." He just kept repeating this is really good news.

I asked if he had ever noticed this before and he said no that he was shocked that I picked out this detail nobody ever saw. I had hopes that scientists would clamor over this footage when I used it in both "Sasquatch Legend Meets Science" and then on "Mysterious Encounters TV series" the first TV series dedicated to the Sasquatch mystery ever on TV. But nope, mostly crickets continued on my little discovery, I am not sure why? I remain hopeful some important field scientists will take note and it will convince him the Sasquatch topic is worthy of study.

A similar situation happened when I discovered what appears to be a hernia on the PGF creature that I thought would help authenticate the 1967 footage. After all, it rises and falls with the correct muscle and leg movement, an injury that even surgeons recognized as a hernia that females get often associated with pregnancy, and the fact the creature in the film had breasts.

I expected next-level discussions on this, and while this new detail quietly does its work amongst people who tend to be open-minded, most hard-core skeptics remain unphased. Hopefully, this book and the wide distribution coupled with further enhanced IBT Freeman baby video that is available below will cause more scientific scrutiny on his footage and the possible infant shown, something Paul Freeman would have relished, he wanted his footage scrutinized scientifically, something hoaxers run from.

Author's Note: According to Vance Orchard in the Touchet Valley Ramblings, Paul Freeman described what he believed to be a second bigfoot in his footage. The bigfoot had what appeared to be a lump or deformity on the side of its neck and face.

Paul saw this creature from approximately one hundred feet away through the trees. At that moment in the footage, the bigfoot appears to be picking up a small juvenile Bigfoot. Could this lump or deformity Freeman described actually be a baby clinging to its mother or lying on her back?

The Enhanced Footage

The Enhanced Second Bigfoot Footage

A track from Scenic Loop in 1995 as followed and documented by Paul and Dar Addington.

7.

NOTES FROM THE FIELD: THE SCENIC LOOP TRACKWAY

January 31 - February 2, 1995

Dar Glasgow Addington

Monday, January 30, 1995

I got a call from Paul Freeman. He said some kids were parked up on the Mormon Grade/Scenic Loop area Saturday night, January 28, and had heard some screaming that really shook them up. So the plan was to go up there the next AM and look for evidence, tracks and other signs. That night it rained and the thought of all the tracks being washed out was grim.

Tuesday, January 31, 1995

I got to Paul's house at 7:30 am and we waited a few minutes for Bill Laughery from the Tri-Cities and Billy Field from Touchet to arrive. By 8:00 we were on our way up to Scenic Loop via 5-mile road. It had stopped raining and there was the chance it hadn't rained too hard up there. We were trying to be optimistic. When we got to the top of Scenic, however, the wind was picking up and it looked like a squall was starting to blow in. Dave Been, who lived in Mill Creek, was already there and had found tracks coming out of the stubble and going along the brush just above where the road turns right and starts down into Mill Creek. I had borrowed a camcorder but the conditions for taping were not good. Trying to walk in the partially frozen, lumpy field, while trying to look through an eyepiece was a joke. The excitement of the trackway kept us all going though.

The brush along the tracks had been snapped off. The shriveled Rosehips and Elderberries had been stripped off and their branches discarded in the field. The tracks came down to the road and then resumed again behind a bush on the other side. They then walked across a small, steep strip, over a saggy barbed wire fence, and into the next big field. The edge of the field drops off sharply here down to Mill Creek. The tracks were not too deep, and some emerging wheat sprouts were flattened in them. After about an hour of intense search Paul, Bill, and Billy turned back. I went on a little

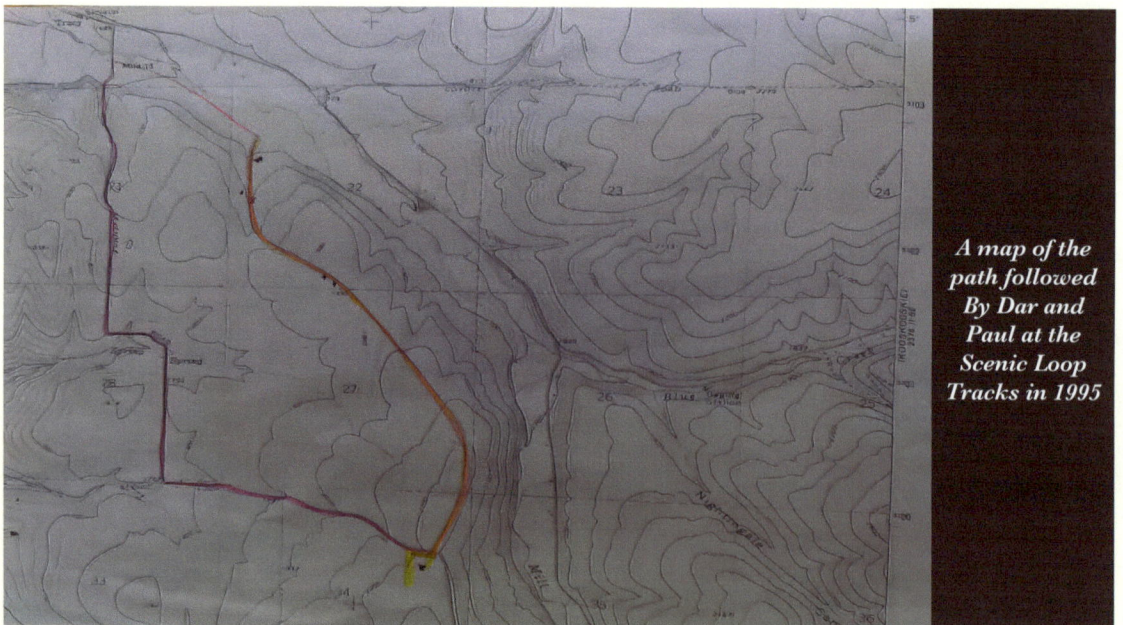

A map of the path followed By Dar and Paul at the Scenic Loop Tracks in 1995

longer with Dave Been. We walked very slowly, looking at the tracks that were faint, but readable. Dave was following a line of tracks about twenty feet above the ones I was following too. Dave's line was angling up and I lost sight of him as I was concentrating on the faint line of track I was following. I came to some large trees and brush. Kind of a thicket at the edge of the field. I saw two sets of tracks coming up out of there, and also a shorter, wider track. I started to go down in there but immediately started to get a feeling of fear and decided that I had gone far enough by myself. It looked like a good spot for a cougar ambush. I came back up and saw Dave. I could hear Geese honking down below and realized we were across from where Blue Creek joins into Mill Creek. Dave's own house with a pond and geese was down there on the other side. Dark clouds were coming and we decided it was time to quit and go back before we got drenched. We walked back across the top of the big field and came out on Scenic Loop near where the vehicles were parked.

Wednesday, February 1, 1995

At 9 AM, I drove back up with a different camera. It wasn't raining, but it was overcast. I wanted to get a few pictures, as the video was a bust. I had my small dog with me for company. We parked on top, crossed the road and followed the lower set of tracks (close to the edge), and took some pictures. They were back from the edge of the field about twenty feet. I found one that had scat in it. On closer inspection, the scat was lots of mouse hair and I could see a prune pit in it. I snapped a pic and tossed it in a baggie. We walked back to the area across from where Blue Creek joins Mill Creek. A whitetail doe was spooked out of there and trotted across the field. I was out of time, so we turned back. We spooked three more whitetails. I could see many deer in the field below Scenic Loop and also a large flock of wild Turkey. I counted twenty-four. There was a helicopter doing some logging in Mill Creek. The creek was running high and fast when I crossed Wickersham bridge on the way home.

Thursday, February 2, 1995

The stormy weather had finally passed. The sun was out and it was a beautiful morning. I called Paul Freeman and said I wanted to go up again, and he said "let's go." I picked him up and we drove up and parked on top of Scenic Loop. We went out across the top where walking was easier and came down by the trees above the Mill Creek/Blue Creek junction and resumed following the faint tracks that were angled off northwest. They were faint and hard to follow. The little tracks would vanish. Paul thought that maybe it might climb up on the bigger one and ride.

The bigger tracks became deeper and shorter going uphill when the smaller ones would disappear, and that's how we came to agree on that theory. I found an apple with bites taken out of it. It was about ten feet from the line of tracks. There were also two places where the tracks stopped, turned facing southwest and then turned back north. We stood behind them and tried to see what they might be looking at. When we got to the last knoll, the tracks shifted back east toward Mill Creek. Then we lost them. They were easy to lose. We circled back and forth, looking. Then Paul called to me and waved. He was about one hundred yards away. I started toward him, watching the ground at every step.

I was very close to him when I saw the big, deep tracks coming across toward the fence line. The land dropped off sharply there. Deep tracks passed under a tree and stopped. Above us. we could see the snapped, broken branch tips, and they were strewn on the ground. The smell of pine pitch was heavy. Briefly, we caught a raunchy small as well. The tracks went off to the east (toward Mill Creek) and over a barbed wire fence that had seen better days. It was old and sagging and flopped over uphill. The bottom wire had a bonanza of soft fluffy reddish blonde hair caught on a barb. I reached out, but Paul said "Don't touch it". He had a pair of hemostats in his pocket. He got out a baggie and picked all the hair off of the barb. We then started making our way down to the flat floodplain area. We both started to have a strong *"let's get out of here"* feeling of danger. On the other side of the creek was Old Coyote Road. We went west toward Seven Mile Bridge.

At this point, Paul's foot was screaming in pain. We got to the road and he sat down by the ditch. He was hurting and could go no further. So I had to leave him there and walk Seven Mile Road back up to Scenic Loop, about four miles away. About a mile up there was the raunchy smell again. It was bad. It was a dead horse lying next to the road. That explained the smell we caught earlier. It stunk in the wind. It might also explain the two places where the tracks had stopped and turned toward the Southwest up top. Could it have been catching the scent of the dead horse? I really don't recommend taking a stroll up Seven Mile Road. It is long and lonely.

No one for miles. No cars passed in either direction the whole way. By the time I got back to the truck, I was exhausted. Surprise, Paul was already there. Someone had seen him sitting by the ditch, picked him up, and driven up Mill Creek Road to Scenic Loop. He just grinned and asked, "What took you so long?"

The Mormon Grade/Scenic Loop Trackway of 1995. There are no known casts from this trackway although it was photographed and documented by numerous individuals. This may have been due to the conditions.

This photo shows the amount of rain that had fallen the night before, and the wet and muddy conditions made it hard to follow the tracks.

Dar Glasgow Addington. Photo by Vance Orchard.

Scat found in a track by Dar Addington at the 1995 Scenic Loop Trackway.

This track which is thought to possibly be of Wrinkle Foot was found later in 1987 at the South Fork of the Walla Walla River area. This creature will end up being one of the most documented individuals in the database.

8.

FAMILY OBSERVATION

Michael Freeman

'm going to be very careful with what I say here. There is a major difference between thinking and knowing, and much of what I'm about to propose is, at least at this moment, my thinking. My thoughts do not necessarily reflect the opinions or theories of any of the contributors to this book, and this is simply what I believe was happening at the time. I have taken a lot of time and great care over the years to review and study the Blue Mountain evidence. I have looked at hundreds of photos of tracks found and casts made. I have listened to hours of audio journals and watched hours of video footage. I have done this over and over. I have also spoken at length with individuals more qualified than myself to make print and cast identifications. It is my belief that what we had roaming the Blue Mountains during my father's time of research was a group of Bigfoot that consisted of one adult male, two adult females, and one, possibly two, juvenile individuals. There is a possibility that up to two more adults were in the area during the early to mid-1980s that I do not believe were still present during the 1990s. This is something that is still being analyzed as I continue to work on identifying existing track and cast data.

The study of tracks and casts can be a tricky business. An animal that usually leaves a 14-inch track could be found with one that is now 18 inches. This happens frequently, and there are many variables that can contribute to variances in not only size but also toe position and even foot width. Substrate, weather conditions and terrain are just a few of those factors to be considered. Is the ground hard or soft? Was it wet from rain or snow? Was the animal walking up an incline, or was there a downhill grade? For example, a heavy animal moving quickly down a wet slope could potentially slide with its step and produce a track that appears to be longer than usual, and may even change the position of the toes. Let us not forget after all that footprint is not an image of a foot, but rather the damage that is left due to the foot striking the ground. All of this information along with my father's audio accounts, video logs, other witness accounts, and my own personal experiences have been taken into consideration to form the above opinion.

There are multiple accounts on record of at least two individual bigfoot being present. There were two sets of individual tracks found at Elk Wallow in 1982. At Deduct Spring, my dad tells us there are two of them. By my father's audio account there were two present on October 5th, 1988 when my brother Duane took his photos, and we know there were at least two at the 1995 Scenic Loop trackway, with one presumed to be juvenile. There is also an account of three more sets of tracks being found on June 11th, 1982 from the Search and Rescue team that was deployed to search the area. These tracks were said to be found a quarter of a mile away on a ridge top. There are no photos or casts of these tracks. These are just examples of accounts from the area involving two or more individuals. There are presumably many more than this.

There are juvenile tracks being cast at Gifford Peak in 1992. There is video of this. That video is actually part of the master footage tape the Deduct film is on, although it was shot four months prior and in a different location. My father still had the same tape in the camcorder and was taping over other recordings on that day. There has been more than one person who tried to claim the two footage events are connected, but for the final time, they are not. The tracks cast at Gifford Peak are 8-9 inches. We have tracks then found that are 11-12 inches three years later at Scenic Loop. Could this be the same individual? Or another younger one? Other castings of small "juvenile" tracks were also made by not only my father but others in the area as well during this time. We know there was at least one juvie in the area. There is also a possibility that there was one that was much younger. That possibility is being actively studied from at least one piece of my father's evidence at this time and seems more and more likely with every new enhancement.

Wrinkle Foot is about a 14-inch track, with possible tracks up to 18 inches where the foot may have slid with the step. Some of these tracks are still being identified and matched to individuals, so I will use the term possible. The track size of Wrinkle Foot had not grown over the years, so I can assume that the individual was fully grown. Based on the track size I will agree with Professor Krantz that this is a female. "She" is a widely documented individual in the database with numerous tracks found and cast in 1984, 1987 and 1988. There is also the possibility she may be responsible for some tracks seen in 1982, and also as late as 1992. This is currently being studied in hopes of a positive identification match in both cases.

The other individual that I believe may be a female is the one Wes Sumerlin may have nicknamed "Big Jim". I will refer to her as female #2 (Big Jill?). This individual's tracks were the ones found at the 1991 Mill Creek Road trackway and are roughly 13.5 inches. At this point, her tracks had been seen for many years already, and this same individual would again be cast in 1996 by Dr. Jeff Meldrum. With the track size remaining within a half inch the same, I again will assume it is fully grown based on that track size, and also a female. This may also be one of the individual's found at the 1995 Scenic Loop Trackway, which is in the same general area as both the 1991 tracks and 1996 tracks mentioned above. Again, I will clarify that I think it may be and am currently working on this identification as well.

Left to discuss are the 17-18 inch tracks found by Freeman in 1987, and possibly on at least one other occasion (I say possibly here because this track data has not been fully documented). This is obviously a large individual. I believe this is a male. He is also very elusive and is by far the least documented of what I believe to be the three adults in the group.

Observation

An analysis of the tracks filmed in the "Freeman Footage" is underway. Even to this day, there is still much studying to be done on the footage, and video stills are being compared to existing tracks in the database. I along with Cliff Barackman and Jeff Meldrum are in agreement though that these tracks are the same as Female #2, and the same individual we have from both 1991 Mill Creek Road and 1996 Five Points. Despite the massive size that the animal appears to be in the video, I would be surprised if she is over 6'7" or 6'8" and may be smaller. I am again basing this off of track size at 13.5-14 inches and my belief that the females would be smaller than the males. Let us not forget that Grover Krantz was estimating "Patty" at 6'6" when everyone thought she would be well over seven feet tall.

We now know, or think I should say, that "Patty" is probably 6'6" at max, with a track about a half inch larger than the Freeman subject. I'm not sure I personally trust the reports of ten-foot (or Larger) sasquatch. Not that I don't believe the accounts, I would never diminish a person's Bigfoot sighting, but rather I think the size is overestimated due to the human brain's reaction to shock and fear, not to mention distance. Even my father, who after his first sighting in 1982 initially thought the creature may be nine feet tall, would say later, after a few more sightings, that it was probably more around seven feet. Our big male here with a track of 17 inches may not be more than seven and a half feet tall. Some will disagree with me here, maybe even a scientist or two, but again, this is my opinion and it is based on the information I have and what I believe to be most likely plausible. It seems to me that the impressive part, the impressive size of these creatures is through the chest and shoulders. The individual in the Freeman Footage is quite massive here and I would wager that she is larger in chest circumference than 'Patty" who was once estimated at around sixty inches.

I believe the two females were traveling together with the juvenile(s). I do not know about the big male, he is a bit of a mystery. Perhaps he is following the rest of the group, watching over them from a distance. Perhaps he is scouting ahead, finding a safe route for the others. Perhaps he is not present at all. It is possible he is rogue, mostly sticking to himself, and traveling through different territories only to return when he feels the urge to mate.

I will also not assume to know the family dynamic of the Bigfoot species. The two adult females could be separate individual mates of the male, or perhaps they are sisters. I suppose one could even be an older daughter that is fully grown now and remaining within the group. All three of these could be a possibility, but I do not know, nor will I surmise to know. I will infer though and say that I think all three of the adult individuals would have died by now. My father first cast Wrinkle Foot thirty-eight years ago and she was already a grown adult. We do not know the growth rate or life span of the species, that is guesswork at the moment. But I myself have to think that they have long since perished. The Juvenile(s) could be alive though, possibly. And if not then perhaps there were offspring from it/them that could still be roaming the Blue Mountain area.

Here I will remind you that I am not my father. I am not the tracker that he was, nor have I had a personal sighting. And although I do not have the research experience and expertise that my dad had, I am experienced with the evidence and his research. After all, I was raised in this. We know that my father often referred to the creatures he was tracking as a "little family", and that they were often found or spotted in groups of at least two in that area. We also know there was at least one juvenile based on track finds, and that the two I believe to be females were around for a long time and are both highly documented. So no, I am not Paul Freeman. Not even close. But perhaps I am on the right track(s).

These Damn Things Exist

I will close this section by actively challenging you, the reader, to form your own opinions and theories. Look for yourself at the evidence contained in this book. Compare Tracks and casts. Listen to my father's audio accounts, and watch the videos within. Take all the information provided to you, and use it to do your own research on the Freeman Files. It is, after all, a great mystery. What will your conclusion be?

This track that measures 17 inches was found in 1987. I believe it may be from April, but have limited information on the location. It is most certainly our big male though.

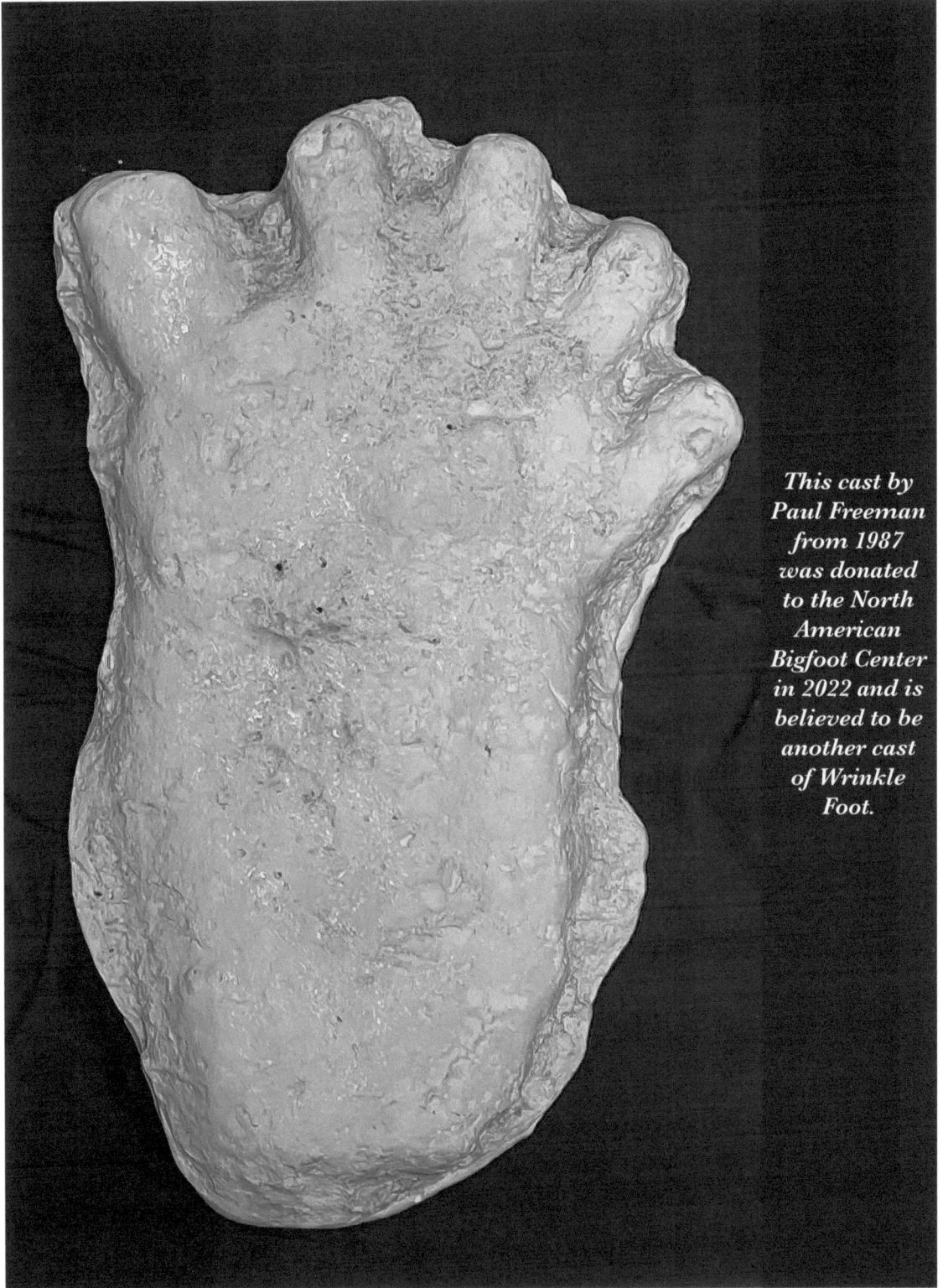

This cast by Paul Freeman from 1987 was donated to the North American Bigfoot Center in 2022 and is believed to be another cast of Wrinkle Foot.

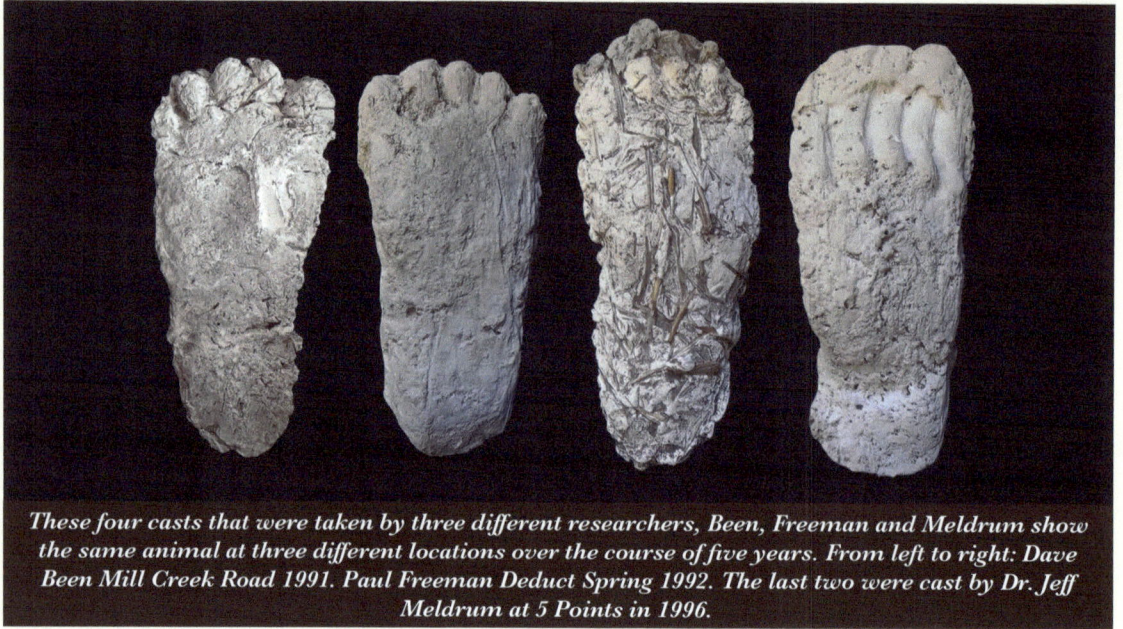

These four casts that were taken by three different researchers, Been, Freeman and Meldrum show the same animal at three different locations over the course of five years. From left to right: Dave Been Mill Creek Road 1991. Paul Freeman Deduct Spring 1992. The last two were cast by Dr. Jeff Meldrum at 5 Points in 1996.

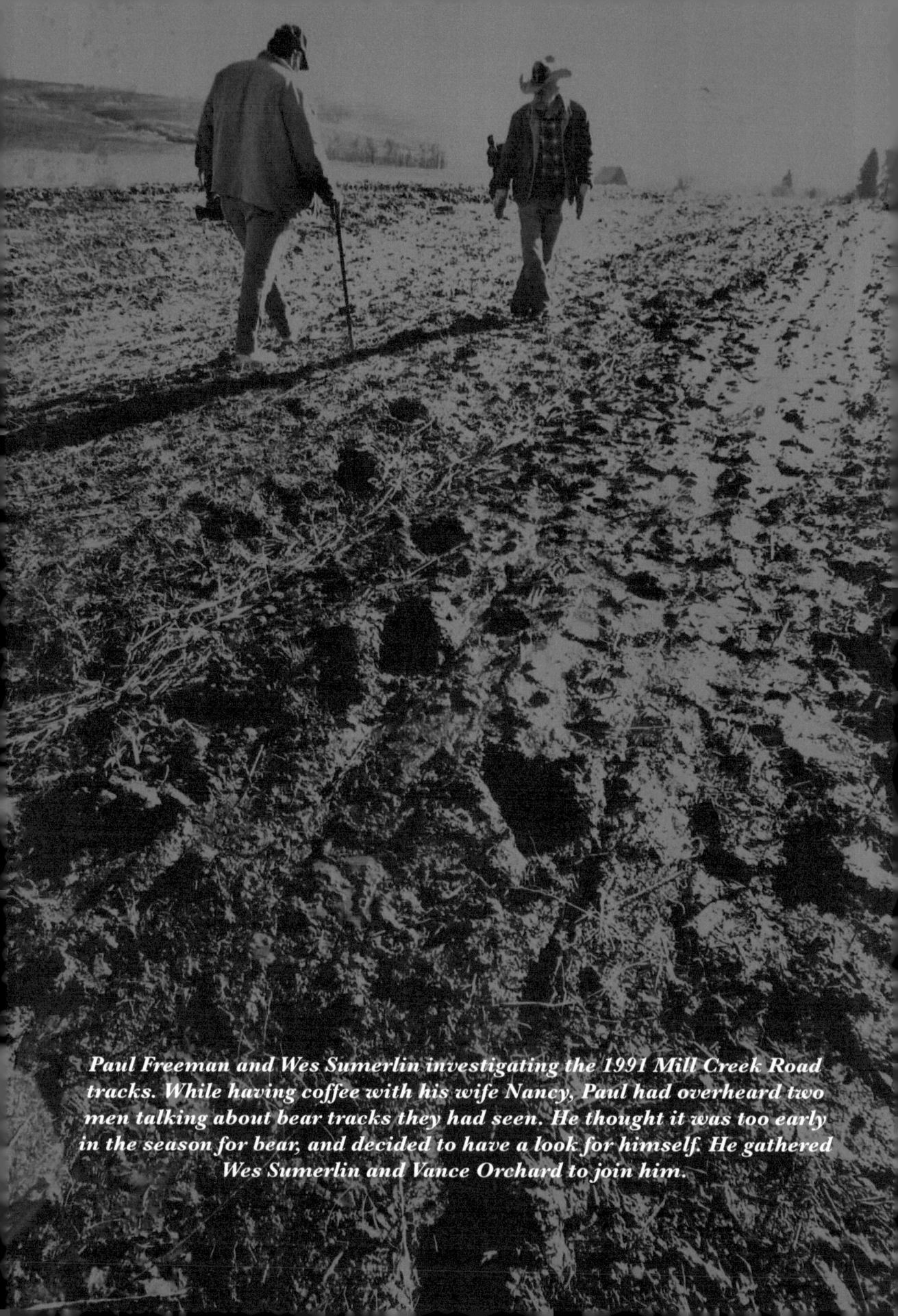

Paul Freeman and Wes Sumerlin investigating the 1991 Mill Creek Road tracks. While having coffee with his wife Nancy, Paul had overheard two men talking about bear tracks they had seen. He thought it was too early in the season for bear, and decided to have a look for himself. He gathered Wes Sumerlin and Vance Orchard to join him.

9.

THE FINAL INTERVIEW

Thom Powell

1943 - 2003

It was more than twenty years ago that I was visited by Paul Freeman and his wife, Nancy. The occasion was an interview for a TV show that was being produced by a documentary crew from Manchester, England. Part of my contribution to this project was to bring Paul Freeman to my place for a taped interview. Later, the crew would pack up and head into Portland for the next interview with Henner Fahrenbach in my middle school classroom.

The English production crew was kind enough to allow me to tape both interviews 'over their shoulder' so to speak, using my own home camcorder. Only a few short clips from these two extended interviews were ever televised in their show. The rest of the interviews ended up on the cutting room floor. My copy of the interviews, on VHS tapes, just sat in a drawer for the next ten years, along with my tape of the discovery of the Skookum Cast.

I finally got around to reformatting these old tapes to a digital format. Despite the generally poor sound quality of my tapes (my fault), I was amazed by the value of reflections and recollections that were offered by both interviewees, Paul Freeman and Henner Fahrenbach. The material on these tapes was as useful as it was ten years ago. I put the tapes up on YouTube because it struck me that anyone who ever has tried or will someday try to gather 'bigfoot evidence' needs to hear every word of these interviews. There is a huge amount of personal experience and 'hard gotten gains' presented in these old tapes.

The Freeman interview is perhaps the most interesting one for a few reasons. First, Paul Freeman died just a year after this interview was taped. So this interview, unbeknownst to me at the time, would be his last, and maybe the longest taped interview of his life. What adds still more interest to the Freeman interview is the fact that controversy swirled around Freeman's name and reputation over the twenty or so years that Freeman was associated with sasquatch matters. But the biggest reason why I feel the Freeman interview is so important is that, if one wants to benefit from somebody else's lifetime of field research, Paul Freeman is your guy. Paul Freeman may be dead but for my money, Paul Freeman is, and always will be the ultimate 'bigfoot field researcher.'

While the term "bigfoot field researcher" is a vague and even sort of a self-anointed title, anyone who ever aspires to be a 'bigfoot field researcher' would do well to click on the links at the end of this essay and listen to every word of these poorly recorded but fascinating video segments.

One interesting element of these tapes is the fact that the English reporter who interviews Freeman had really done his homework. He knew the controversies that Paul was embroiled in and he did his best to get Paul Freeman to articulate his position on the accusations of hoaxing that swirled back in the 1990s. The biggest flap surrounded comments made by Freeman on a "Good Morning America" appearance. He acknowledged "trying to make" a set of fake footprints. Freeman explained to me as we chatted at my house before the interview that his remarks were taken out of context. He wanted to create a set of deliberate fakes for comparison purposes. He never tried to portray the fakes as anything but an experiment. But by acknowledging on camera that he had 'tried' to make fake footprints, he created a dust-up that many would seize upon to cast doubt on any and all evidence ever gathered by this remarkably dedicated field researcher.

As he explains in the interview, Paul Freeman dedicated fifteen years of his life to gathering evidence out of one particular area, the Blue Mountains, and specifically the Mill Creek Watershed, that straddles the border between Washington and Oregon within the Blue Mountains. During these fifteen or so years, Paul Freeman collected what seemed at the time to be an impossible number of and variety of casts. Nobody, it was contended by competing researchers like Dahinden and Byrne, could possibly have that many encounters with such rare and elusive creatures. Freeman was also claiming a handful of eyeball sightings, and then, a brief video clip of a sasquatch.

From the more sophisticated perspective we enjoy today, it's laughable to suggest that Freeman must have been hoaxing his evidence simply because he had so much of it. There are numerous other examples today of people with the kind of multiple encounters that only Freeman was claiming two or three decades ago. The concept of 'habituation' did not even exist in the lexicon of the subject back then, and while it remains highly controversial today, I can state unequivocally from my personal perspective that long-term, repeat encounters with sasquatches certainly do occur. Further, we know now that there are most definitely places where the sasquatch activity is more overt and concentrated than in the rest of the world, and from everything I think I know, Freeman was indeed onto such a 'hot spot'. It was mostly the competing researchers of the time, particularly Dahinden, who felt there was no way Freeman could be onto such a hot spot.

Rene Dahinden was wrong. There are lots of other hot spots we know of today. By today's standard, there is nothing remarkable about the claims of Paul Freeman, especially in light of that fantastic spot that Freeman was working on a regular basis: remote, vast in size, and off-limits to the general public, owing to its role as a municipal drinking water collection watershed. I would further contend that Paul Freeman was fortunate enough to be hunting for evidence not only in the perfect place but at the perfect time. Never before had anyone attempted to gather evidence in that particular large expanse of wilderness that Freeman knew so well from his work as a caretaker of the watershed. This made it much easier for Freeman to find evidence and even to approach the creatures themselves. We know today that the presence of other researchers definitely contaminates an area. Paul Freeman, owing to his experience, to the time period, and to the remoteness of the area he was working, did not have the 'researcher contamination' problem we face today.

Then there's the video. Freeman explains the circumstances in the three-part interview I posted on YouTube, so I will forgo a detailed discussion of that. After listening to Freeman's descriptions again, I see nothing implausible about the circumstances that led to obtaining his brief video. Further, much discussion has been generated over the way Freeman reacts to the sighting on the videotape. Apparently, he wasn't excited enough on the video and this was supposedly indicative of some bad acting that was trying to sell the viewer on a hoaxed 'encounter.' That is patently ridiculous, in my view, for two reasons. First, Freeman was sufficiently experienced that I would not expect the same level of excitement to come from him as might emanate from someone who bumped into a creature that they didn't even know existed. Freeman was hunting for a sasquatch with his camcorder that day and to his surprise, he found one right where he expected it to be, precisely the way Patterson and Gimlin happened across one that they managed to film with a 16mm movie camera. But beyond all this, it is clear to me after watching the raw video footage Freeman made, that he is very excited, as well as winded, and a little bit scared.

Most importantly, I have studied the Freeman footage carefully and after overlaying it atop everything I think I know about the sasquatch, I can unequivocally state that the Paul Freeman footage is the real deal. I direct anyone who questions this to several specifics that are generally overlooked by viewers of Paul Freeman's footage:

1. The subject of the Freeman footage is atypical in appearance. It either has a big belly or it is a pregnant female. He shows two sets of tracks on the video, one being smaller and presumably belonging to a juvenile. Freeman speculates that he is tracking a pregnant female with a young one in tow. I doubt that a hoaxer would add such embellishments for fear that they would cast further doubt on an already questionable image.

2. The subject of the footage does something strange. Just as Freeman utters his comment, "There he goes! " the subject steps behind one tree, then emerges from behind another tree about three feet distant, yet one never sees the creature's outline cross the gap between these two trees. Some have supposed that the creature bent down and then stood back up, but I see no sign of this in

the video. Others suggest that the gap between the two trees actually is occupied by another tree. I think I'm seeing an open space between the trees, but I admit I am uncertain on this point. Call me paranormal, but it looks like something really strange is going on in that little segment of the footage.

3.   There's nothing paranormal about the quick look the subject throws toward the camera around the 3:13 mark in the footage. It's a really quick flick of the head toward the camera and that look tells me loud and clear that it's not a guy in a suit. A move that fast would send a costume mask spinning apart from the head inside the mask. That doesn't happen. The video clearly shows a quick flick of a real head by a very coordinated being.

4.   A couple of seconds later, Freeman utters, "Jesus!" as the subject steps behind a small grand fir tree and stops. The subject perfectly positions itself behind the small tree, and then stops moving, rendering it indistinguishable from the tree in front of it. During the couple of seconds when the subject is behind the tree, it cannot be seen at all until it begins to move again. This speaks volumes about the subject and the veracity of Freeman's footage. It reveals a real creature that knew exactly how to conceal itself in plain sight by stepping behind a bush and then standing completely still. It moves, presumably because it understood that Freeman was continuing to approach its location. More than anything else about the Freeman footage, I find this element of the footage to be an impressive display of behavior and intelligence that speaks volumes about how these beings are able to conceal themselves in plain sight.

Call me a sucker, but I'm convinced that Paul Freeman's video clip is absolutely genuine, and it is second only to the Patterson-Gimlin footage (PGF) in terms of image quality. The Freeman footage may actually be superior to the PGF in terms of providing us a window on certain important behaviors, specifically the way that a sasquatch can use the available foliage to instantly conceal itself.

Then there's the interview. Freeman presents, in my view, a very relaxed and highly credible persona. He articulates his position, he speaks with a casual yet confident demeanor that bespeaks a man who is firmly in possession of a lifetime of woodsman experience. He dismisses his detractors without a hint of animosity, and he matter-of-factly issues an open invitation for anyone to show where and why his video footage is fake. He acknowledges that the body of evidence he has gathered is not utterly compelling but he stands by the veracity and integrity of everything he has collected.

I wasn't sure what to expect when I was setting up the interview with Paul Freeman, but I came away impressed. But two other events that are not seen in the taped interview I posted on YouTube removed all doubt in my mind about the truthfulness and integrity of Paul Freeman.

First, Paul's wife Nancy sat there on the sofa in my living room sofa face-to-face during the entire interview. When he described in the interview the way his wife ("the boss") forbid him from putting a bigfoot scat in the oven to dry it, he's looking right at her. That spoke volumes about the man's credibility. If a guy is going to sit there and tell lies, I don't think he would do so with his wife sitting there in the same room, looking him square in the eye.

Even more amazing, when the interview was over, Paul gathered up all the track casts and the handprint cast and handed them to me. "Here," he said. "I want you to have these."

I thought I misunderstood him. "Do you want to sell me these things?" I asked.
"No. I want you to have them."
"But these are worth a lot of money...," I stammered
" I don't want money."
"Shouldn't they at least be a part of some scientific collection?"
"I sent a trailer full of stuff to Dr. Meldrum. There's plenty of my stuff in scientific collections. You're a science teacher. I'm going to die soon. After I'm gone, I just want some of this stuff to be shown around to kids. Will you do that for me?"
How can one not be impressed by that?

Fifteen months later, Paul Freeman did die. I've tried to keep my end of the bargain, so every year I show the 8th graders the artifacts Paul collected. Since bigfoot isn't really an accepted part of Portland's official science curriculum, I show it on the day before Spring Break, when a third of the class has already left for Hawaii. We talk about standards of evidence and what constitutes scientific proof of undocumented species. Like grown-ups, most kids dismiss Paul's evidence as fake. I understand the need to keep the concept of 'bigfoot' at a distance, especially in the minds of kids. I don't push it and I don't tell them everything I know.

And another thing I don't push is my feeling that Paul Freeman IS the genuine article; the ultimate bigfoot field researcher. His video is real and it shows a real creature. It is my view that Paul Freeman made as big a contribution to our current understanding of the bigfoot phenomenon as anyone, ever. So, I posted the 'lost tapes' of his interview on YouTube in the hope that other aspiring field researchers the world over can learn as much as I learned from the legacy of Paul Freeman, The Ultimate Field Man.

Interview with Paul Freeman (Part 1)

Interview with Paul Freeman (Part 2)

A rare photograph of Nancy Freeman on site. 1987.

10.

THE END

Michael Freeman

Paul Freeman would walk away from his search for Bigfoot in 1997. The stress on his marriage and his bank account had become too much. And although he wouldn't admit it at the time, his health was declining rapidly, and he was tired. He packed my mother up and moved her to somewhere she always wanted to be, Long Beach, Washington. Part of her family lived there, and that woman loved the beach. Nancy Freeman was happier. Paul Freeman was dying. The foot that he had injured so many years ago and had required so many surgeries, was failing him. He was in constant pain and was having trouble walking. His blood pressure had gotten worse along with his diabetes, and he was gaining weight. The worst decision my father made in his life was letting a doctor talk him into having that foot amputated. They said it would be better, easier to walk with a prosthetic, and less pain. All it did was take his soul away. His weight made it difficult to learn to walk with a prosthetic, and the wound from the procedure wasn't healing correctly. He could no longer go to the mountains and hike. He could no longer walk to hunt. By the time of his death, he could barely make it to the water's edge to get a fishing line in, and he was spending more and more time in a wheelchair.

My father's body died just outside of Spokane, in Airway Heights Washington, but I know his heart died in that wheelchair. His decline is the most depressing thing I've ever witnessed, and it haunts me. You would think that the saddest memory I have of my father is his death, but it is not. That memory came just over three months prior to his death when I came to visit my parents for Christmas. When I got home my dad tried to give me a bear hug and pick me up. This giant of a man who was my hero when I was a child now limped across the floor and could no longer lift me. I know that hurt and embarrassed him deeply, and that broke my heart. The toughest man I have ever known was gone.

Mountain Man's Paradise

My father knew he was going to die. He told Thom Powell fifteen months before his death that he wouldn't live much longer. That was the last interview he would ever give. The last doctor's appointment my father had was the first time in their lives together that he would not allow my mother to go back in the room with him. After thirty-six years of marriage, she was made to sit in the waiting room for the first and only time. At that moment she knew as well. Shortly after that, they took a long drive together. I don't know the details of what was discussed, but I know that almost forty years of life together, and stress, and fights, and most importantly love were put on the table. I never saw my parents disagree again.

When I'm An Old Man

Paul Freeman died at his home on April 02, 2003. He was fifty-nine years old, and it was snowing. His wife and youngest boy were at home with him. He was married to Nancy Freeman for thirty-six years, and together they had three children. He was a great man.

Raw Footage Shot by Paul Freeman

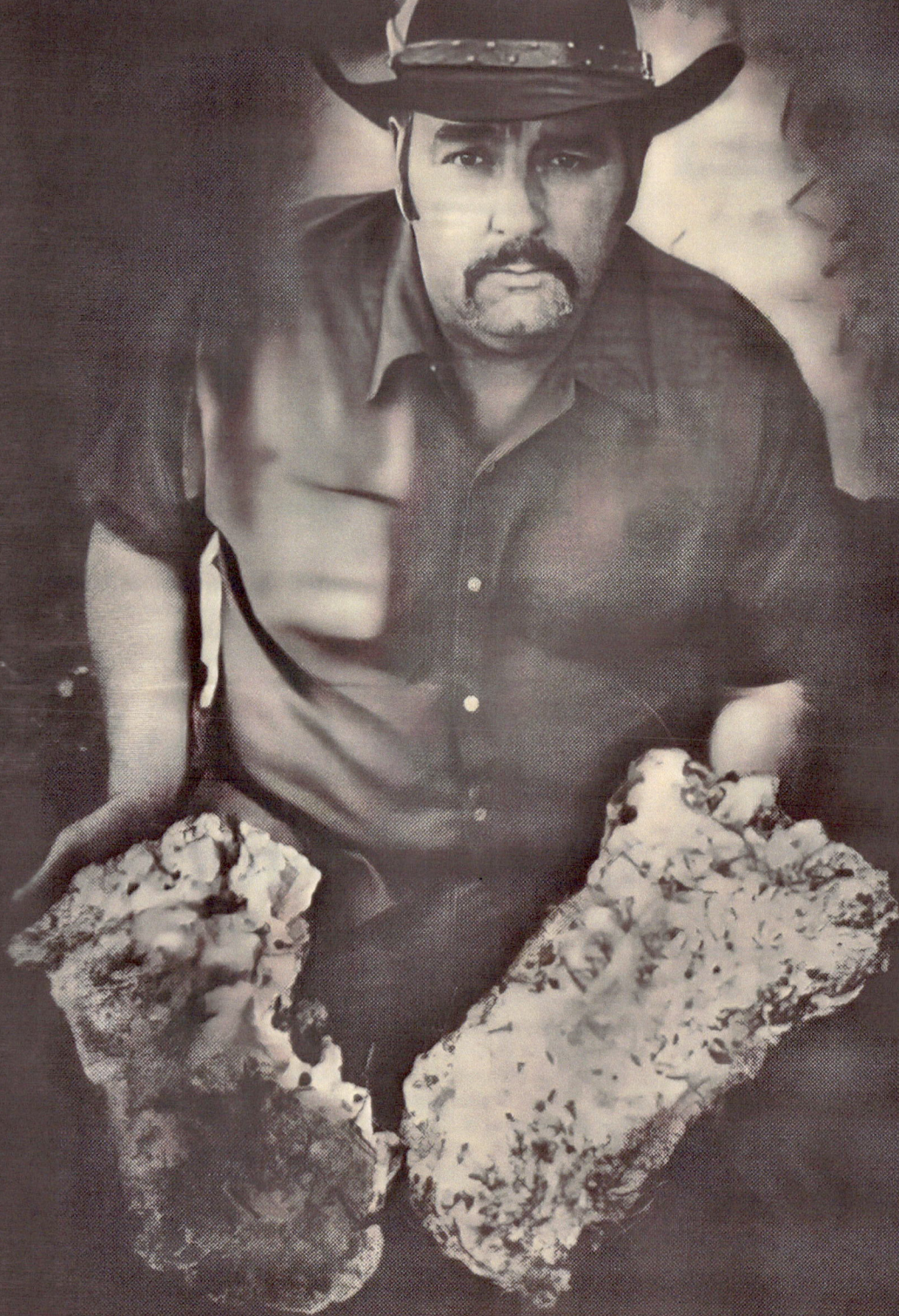

Paul shows off tracks he found for the Walla Walla union bulletin in 1987.

Bigfoot hunter Paul Freeman shows plaster casts made from his discovery of footprints in the Blue Mountains last week. Freeman said one of the tracks measured nearly 17 inches long and 9 inches wide. Greg May, pictured at right, from the Pullman-based "Bigfoot Expedition 1," came to Walla Walla after hearing about the footprints found by Freeman.

II.

BONUS AUDIO SECTION

Intro Full

Joel Hardin

Paul Freeman Speaking at a Western Bigfoot Society Meeting

Douglas WY

Tickled Pink

The Best Evidence In The World

AFTERWORD

Go to hangar1publishing.com to learn more about the Author and stay up to date with their newest releases.

BIOGRAPHY

Michael Freeman was born on February 2nd, 1977 in Vancouver, Washington. He has been working as a professional gymnastics coach for over twenty years, and currently resides in Spokane Washington along with his wife Whitney and their three sons.

Paul and Nancy Freeman in front of their Deli "Freeman's" in Camas, Washington 1984-85.

www.ingramcontent.com/pod-product-compliance
Lightning Source LLC
Chambersburg PA
CBHW041547260326
41914CB00016B/1579

9 781955 471657